how to start a home-based

DJ Business

how to start a home-based

DJ Business

Joe Shambro

gpp®

Guilford, Connecticut

For Doug

To buy books in quantity for corporate use
or incentives, call **(800) 962–0973**
or e-mail **premiums@GlobePequot.com**.

Editorial Director: Cynthia Hughes Cullen
Editor: Tracee Williams
Text Design: Sheryl P. Kober
Layout: Casey Shain
Diagram on page 87 by Lori Enik

ISSN 2163-8772
ISBN 978-0-7627-7318-3

Printed in the United States of America
10 9 8 7 6 5 4 3 2 1

This book's purpose is to provide accurate and authoritative information on the topics covered. It is sold with the understanding that neither the author nor the publisher is engaged in rendering legal, financial, accounting, and other professional services. Neither Globe Pequot Press nor the author assumes any liability resulting from action taken based on the information included herein. Mention of a company name does not constitute endorsement.

Contents

Acknowledgments

A very special thank you to all of the small business owners and mobile DJ professionals who offered their advice for this book. Much of the advice and must-haves of the DJ business mentioned in this book came as a result of their hard work and self-admitted mistakes over the years.

Special thanks to the incredible Tracee Williams at Globe Pequot Press for her Zen-like patience and incredibly valuable advice and assistance in making this book happen.

Introduction

Everybody has a favorite memory when thinking of a DJ. Whether it's watching a relative dance an awkward "Electric Slide" or a bride and groom performing their first dance to an unfortunately chosen '80s hair ballad, there's been recorded music as entertainment at many of your life's most fun events. I've still got the video of my grandmother holding up an entire procession of line dancers at my cousin's wedding—and might I add the DJ handled it gracefully. It is memories like these that come with a professional DJ attached. And you have probably attended some events that were ruined by bad DJs and even by your biggest competitors, live bands—and those events would have been saved if a good, professional DJ like you're hoping to be had been there to provide the beat and work the crowd. Professional DJs are a rapidly growing, highly profitable business that has no shortage of customers at all price points.

Starting a new business is, for some people, a paralyzing proposition. Giving up your stable paycheck and benefits can be really frightening. Safety nets are a nice thing to have, and unfortunately, many small business owners don't have one. That's where a book like this comes in. While you might have a great ear for music, a love for energizing a celebrating crowd, and a desire to make money at something you love, starting a business is a lot more difficult than just gathering some gear and reaching out to customers. There are a lot of things you need to do before you ever hit the decks for your first gig—you need to set up your business's legal structure, manage your finances, and make sure all of your insurance and licensing are up to date. You'll have to be prepared for dealing with your customers, your competitors, event guests, and know when you're getting a bad deal, both as a DJ pro and a business owner. You'll need to learn how to adapt your show to meet different, diverse clients, and you also should be comfortable handling business negotiations behind-the-scenes, especially when things go bad. Last but not least, you'll have to become very familiar with the tax structure of running a small business. None of this is easy, and there's no one-size-fits-all approach. That makes starting a business a complicated and highly personal endeavor.

Learning about your clients, their likes and dislikes, and the best way to market your product to them is the biggest part of your new job that will require the most guesswork and research on your part. Whether it's playing top 40 hits (the clean edits, at least) at a high school dance or spinning country all night at a wedding reception, you'll need to be a Swiss Army knife of entertainment in order to stay viable. While a lot of your gigs will be dances and parties, as a new DJ, you'll be spending a lot of time at weddings—they'll be your biggest payday gigs, and after you gain a solid reputation as a good wedding DJ, the gigs will be coming in faster than you can take them. That's assuming you run your business well and offer a professional-level product. Everybody knows a "friend of a friend" who knows how to DJ, and you'll never be able to meet those friends-and-family prices. Being a standout in your community, pricing yourself fairly, and offering an excellent experience for your clients and their guests is the best path to success.

Starting any business is hard. It's expensive and time-consuming, and there's a lot of personal stress and financial investment involved. With a solid knowledge of the DJ business and an understanding of how to run a successful business, you'll be in great shape to jump right in and start taking on paid clientele. Taking the time to start a business properly seems like the long way around, but you'll be glad you put in the time and effort later on when your business is running smoothly (and profitably). Get ready for one of the most stressful and simultaneously rewarding experiences in the world—running your own DJ business.

Let's get started!

01 | Let's Start a DJ Business

Just for a second, let's forget what kind of business you're starting and talk about self-employment in general. Starting a business is a really difficult task—one that eats up and swallows many well-meaning people every year. What does being self-employed mean to you? To some, it's a chance to abandon a desk that they've lived behind for one day too long. For others, it's being able to write their own schedule while following a passion. And for some, self-employment can even be an effective survival tactic in this turbulent economy that's consumed so many good jobs the last few years. Flexibility is one of the main benefits of being your own boss!

Starting your own DJ business is going to be hard. But keep this in mind: Even though you're going into an in-demand and constantly evolving business where you're going to have a lot of fun, there's also a lot of hard work behind the scenes. There's a reason why the other self-employed people I know are some of the toughest people anywhere: It's going to be a lot of hours of work, a lot of time sitting around waiting for your customers to start pouring in, and adjusting to both the benefits and the drawbacks of being self-employed, even part-time, isn't going to be easy, either.

In this chapter, we'll be talking about the joys—and downfalls—of being your own boss. I know, I know—you bought this book to learn the inside track to succeeding specifically in the DJ business, so this might seem like repetition—but trust me. You'll want to learn how to be the consummate self-employed professional alongside how to "hit the decks" like a pro.

Self-Employment and You

My first months of being a self-employed person were a disaster. I'm not afraid to admit that—we all start somewhere, right? Somewhere between waking up past noon every day and not showering until sometime immediately before dinner, I realized that I wasn't living the life of a self-employed person—I was acting as though I was living the life of somebody who's got independent wealth and a reason to sit around and be unproductive. Being self-employed isn't easy, and it takes a lot more work than you might think.

Being successful as a self-employed person means a lot of discipline. It means a lot of hard work and a lot of behind-the-scenes hassle that's not nearly as much fun as being a DJ. Learning your right combination of what makes your business run successfully while providing you, personally, with a high level of satisfaction is something that will likely take some time. It's also highly dependent upon your personal situation, so there's no one-size-fits-all cure. Keep your head in the game, and you'll find success a lot easier to come by.

Are You Ready to be a DJ?

How long have you been interested in being a DJ with your own small business? How much experience do you have behind the decks? According to one survey of self-employed business owners, 65 percent have more than ten years' experience when it comes to their chosen field; 37 percent of those people have almost twenty years of experience. Self-employment has room for people of all skill levels but keeps your skills as sharp as possible. Competing with other small businesses means a lot of brainpower out there—along with a lot of ambitious businesspeople like you trying to make a living with something they love best.

Balancing Work and Family

Before becoming self-employed, you should ask yourself about your personal priorities. Starting your own business, even one as fun as a DJ business, can mean a lot of work, and a lot of time away from home. Depending on your clientele, your schedule will change a lot; you might be DJing a corporate party one afternoon followed by weddings throughout the weekend—all night long. And don't forget the set-up and tear-down time that will come with every gig, too—that's where you start adding on the real time-consuming activities.

One of the reasons why most self-employed individuals choose this path for themselves is their family obligations. Whether you've got kids or aging relatives to care for or are just looking forward to being able to plan on more time to spend with your significant other, being self-employed can give the flexibility you seek. Being your own boss is an amazing, liberating experience—but it's also one that'll scare the pants off of you when you realize just how much work is involved. Just keep this in mind: Finding that right balance is going to be hard, and it's going to take a lot of work. Don't let that discourage you! Being able to properly balance work and family as a newly self-employed person will be a huge key to your overall happiness and success in your new venture.

Although it's safe to say that most of your work will take you outside the home, there's a lot of behind-the-scenes work that you'll be doing—and being able to cope with having work and family so close together is an issue that many self-employed people have to deal with. Not having a separation between your personal life and your work life can be stressful—and it's something that can kill relationships even if you thought that going self-employed would have the opposite effect.

So, as a newly self-employed person, how can you make sure that your family life and your newfound work responsibilities don't clash? I asked several of my self-employed friends, and we came up with the checklist on page 5 based on our experiences. Remember that every situation is unique—but these are some general rules that some successful self-employed people live by.

What "Self-Employed" Really Means

Where did you come from before deciding to start your own DJ business? What line of work were you in? Being newly self-employed means juggling a lot of things—discipline, as we talked about earlier, being the biggest of them. If you're coming into the land of the self-employed after time working behind a desk or mastering a trade, you've probably gotten used to the daily 9-to-5 grind that comes with those types of jobs. You've also undoubtedly gotten used to the fact that you're easily able to leave work at work; after your quitting time rolls around, you clock out, and that's it until tomorrow. And what about the amazing benefits of working a salaried job—health insurance, steady paychecks, and all the other benefits that you'll surely miss when they're not there. Those benefits, and the overall stability of having a "real" job, go right out the window the day you open your business, and all of that responsibility for keeping the ship sailing smoothly falls directly on your shoulders—if you don't do it, it doesn't get done. Sure, it's a heck of a lot of pressure for one person, but that's par for the course.

Being self-employed, even in such an energetic, fun business as DJing, means you've got to take everything head-on. It also means becoming an expert at

Checklist for Managing Your Time

❏ **Make your schedules weekly and stick to them.** But build in time and come up with a plan when you need to take time away for emergencies.

❏ **Give yourself a start time and an end time, just like a regular job.** Even if you're spending six to eight hours a day making phone calls, giving clients quotes, and visiting with potential clients at their event space, make sure you have a time you're willing to quote as your ending time. Yes, you'll need to put in a lot of off-hours work, especially because your clients won't generally need you during normal 9-to-5 business hours. Still, make a schedule and stick to it—that'll give you and your loved ones some normalcy.

❏ **Know when to put work away at home.** You're probably going to be tempted to bring work "home," even for a home-based business. I know it's tempting to always be obsessing over drawing up contracts, making schedules, and organizing your music library for your DJ sets; avoid the lure of catching up during your off-time, if you can.

❏ **Stay motivated.** On the opposite end of the spectrum, it's really hard to stay motivated if you're in a comfortable environment. Learn how to keep yourself motivated in your home office. Put away the distractions and find a way to keep your virtual blinders on (I always had a weakness for being distracted by TNT's daily *ER* rerun every morning). Whether that means getting up first thing in the morning, getting in a workout or a cup of coffee, then starting your day—whatever your routine, stay focused and awake.

❏ **Don't overdo it.** Working yourself to death can feel like the right thing to do, but keep your overall health in mind. As a DJ, you're the life of the party—the central focus that's responsible for keeping the dance floor moving and the event's customers feeling good. They're going to pick up on your mood if you're exhausted (or, worse, hung over). Don't overdo it while working throughout the week, gearing up for your important weekend gigs, and make sure that you're in top shape whenever you're coming face-to-face with a client.

managing your time and resources in ways you never would have thought necessary. There's a lot to do behind the scenes to make sure your business runs smoothly:

- Take care of advertising and marketing, including social and industry networking; this is one of the easiest things to do in today's Internet-based advertising world, but don't let it fool you! Marketing still takes time and a lot of patience.
- Be your own paralegal, which includes taxes and local business law.
- Dedicate time to customer service, from quotes and specs for potential clients to customer complaints (yes, we all have them).
- Manage your business's complex finances, including billing clients.

Being a full-time self-employed person has another complication: Those benefits that come from being employed by a large business suddenly disappear—and your family might depend on them. Whether you were working in the IT industry with its famous officewide perks or just receiving a nice salary, retirement savings, and health-care insurance from a local or regional company, your benefits package is likely to change. Being self-employed means that you're going to have to find (and fund) your own benefits, and this can be a daunting task. We'll talk more about specific aspects later—including the big-ticket items such as retirement savings and health insurance—but rest assured that even the biggest tech company with in-house dog walkers and gourmet lunch-hour chefs can't, ultimately, hold up to being able to set your own schedule, do work on your outdoor patio on a nice day, or simply take a well-deserved day off in the middle of a stressful week if your resources allow it—without having to ask the boss.

Being self-employed isn't for the faint-hearted, and it isn't for everybody—but the rewards can be outstanding if you're able to put the work into it. And although a certain amount of freedom comes from self-employment, it's also a ton of responsibility.

So, how confident are you that being self-employed is right for you? I'm sure that you, as an aspiring professional DJ, are eager to dive in and get started. But keep this in mind: Running a small business isn't for everybody. It takes a specific motivation to stay on task and run your business's finances properly.

Are You Ready for Self-Employment?

Being a self-employed person is a difficult proposition if you're coming from the 9-to-5 work-force. There's a lot to balance, and it's never easy. A lot of small business owners—from myself to the deli owner I buy coffee from daily to the DJs I consulted in this book—had to make a calculated decision on if self-employment was for them. Here's a small worksheet to help you get your numbers in front of your face and let you make some educated calculations. Don't feel bad if the answer is "no, you can't do this right now"—you can always work your way up.

Add up the items requested in the "Cost." This should give you a good financial picture of what your true liabilities as a new business will be—and what your previous job was supplying you in comparison. You'll need to meet these monthly numbers with your business—your salary included—in order to be ready to be fully self-employed.

Monthly Income or Expense	Cost
Ends-Meet Point (your needed salary)	
Health Insurance (actual cost to you)	
Personal Bills (credit cards, etc.)	
Household Expenses	
Car and Transportation Expenses	
Business Expenses	
Monthly Savings Goal	
Total Amount of Monthly Needs	

Knowing When to Quit—And the Risks of Not Listening

Although we're optimistically starting to talk about the rewards of being a full-time self-employed person, there's also a lot of risk, the biggest of which is financial devastation from failure. I've seen it happen, and I've been lucky to not have experienced it myself. Knowing when to quit is one of the biggest things you need to know before starting your own business.

I know, I know—it's depressing to even think about at this early stage in the game. You're filled with optimism and a newly found fire to hit the streets with your new DJ business. But keep this in the back of your mind: You should always set a goal for yourself and stick to it. If you can't meet your goals, and you're falling behind financially and emotionally, it's probably time to step back—and you should always develop your endgame way before it ever becomes necessary. Letting a small business fall into neglect can mean a lot of bad things for you, personally—it can ruin your credit, it can leave you in financial ruin, and it can leave you with a lot of problems if you should want to open a business again in the future.

Later we'll talk about developing that business endgame—what happens when it's time to pack it up. For now, though, let's start putting together your DJ business—with an optimistic eye to the future. Just keep in the back of your mind what your quitting point is—the point where your new business is more burden than it's worth and where you'll need to consider closing up shop. Having this in mind will make that hard decision easier if the time should come.

02 Your DJ Business

I'm assuming if you've made it to Chapter 2, I haven't scared you off yet—and you're still interested in starting your DJ business. Congratulations—you're joining fine company. There are thousands of professional DJs around the world, and it's no secret that pro-level DJing is a multimillion-dollar industry. It's easy to see why—DJs are versatile, they're entertaining, and they truly do offer the best bang for the buck when it comes to entertaining a large number of diverse people. That's going to be your secret to success as the consummate professional DJ—your services are at a premium because of that flexibility and diversity, not to mention your ability to be flexible with your clients' budgets.

So, Why Is a DJ Business Such a Good Idea?

One look at any of my friends' iPods reveals a good indicator of why DJs are the top form of entertainment for weddings and private events worldwide. Musical tastes are as varied as people themselves—one person's tastes may go from Top 40 to jazz to hip hop all in a single playlist; think about that much musical diversity spread out among a guest list of four hundred people. You've got people who live their whole lives immersed in music, and you've got people whose musical interests go no further than the local Top 40 pop station. There's also the performance aspect—many of your well-paying clients want you to be the center of attention, to help move the party along; they want you to be the person responsible for getting their guests into party mode and to be the one to play "bad guy" when it's time to wrap up the festivities. As a DJ, you've got a lot of hats to wear.

Before you jump in to grab your piece of the DJ market, there's a lot of work you have to do to officially set up your business. The first task is defining what your business is, what your business does, and how you're going to do everything. There's also a lot on your plate as a new small business owner—and as you get started, you'll probably notice that there's no tried-and-true formula for a business's success. We'll find your business and personal strengths, we'll find your weaknesses, and we'll figure out how to best balance the needs of a growing business with your personal necessities. From there, we'll write a business plan—an important document that you'll reference (and change) often—then get to the more fun stuff!

Your Time Frame

Many years ago I thought that I'd test my fine entrepreneurial skills—I had always thought I had what it takes to run my own business. After all, I was seven years old, and my father had lovingly grown a brilliant assortment of tomatoes and other summertime vegetables in our backyard. One day—while both parents were at work—I went outside, harvested the best candidates, and set up shop in our driveway selling tomatoes to passersby. The business, for the one day I ran it, was a success—I was so happy I made a few bucks. My dad was livid. But even back then, the worst part of running a small business—even as micro-sized as that one—was the wait for customers to show up.

Years later as an adult, on the day I decided to open my own business, I was incredibly eager to get started serving my clients (and writing myself a paycheck). I remember sitting around and waiting—and waiting, waiting, waiting. That's probably one of the most demoralizing aspects of owning your own business—the wait. It's not just about the frustration of not having any paid work; you're also watching your business's resources drain quickly. But if you think things through from the beginning, your chances of success will be much greater. Still, a lot of outside elements can affect the time frame that it takes for your business to grow and succeed. Simply starting a business isn't enough—and it might not all happen in a day, a week, or even a month. That's why we need to talk about the time frame in which you should expect everything to happen.

Establishing a time frame for your DJ business isn't necessarily about reaching specific goals on a specific schedule, although that's important as well. Finding your timeline is an important tactic when starting your business because it's about pacing yourself in search of those goals that will bring you success. Many businesses have failed because they ran out of money too quickly, and many businesses hit a slow period because they blow their advertising budget for the whole year in the first couple of months (I have been guilty of this in the past).

Establishing a working timeline is absolutely essential to the smooth operation of your growing business. Although you're probably just starting to realize how in-depth this business-owner thing really is, it's important to think long-term as well. You've got a few turbulent months ahead of you, so it's best if you plan your resources accordingly.

Here are a few questions you might want to ask yourself when figuring out how far your finances and resources will go. Doing this will help you establish a budget—very important when we talk about your business plan later on.

How much money—cash and credit—will you have to use from the day you begin your business after major business start-up expenses? We'll call this your "day 1 operating budget."

_____

How much do you plan to budget for marketing expenses per month?

_____

What's your budget per advertising campaign?

_____

When do your business loans, if any, become due?

_____

_____

_____

What are your monthly fixed expenses—both business and personal—that you're responsible for?

_____

_____

_____

Day 1 operating budget:

_____

Day 1 operating budget divided by 12:

_____

Answering these questions will give you the amount of money your business has to sustain itself on for a year's time. That's assuming you don't have any paying clients which is a very unlikely scenario but one that's not unheard of in a small businesses. This amount should give you a good idea of how healthy your business's overall financial picture is for the time being. It'll also give you an idea of how carefully you may need to budget to make sure your business (and personal) fixed expenses are met.

First, let's look at the amount of money you have available. Whether you choose to finance your business through savings, loans, or credit cards, you'll have a finite amount of money that you will start with. We'll assume a worst-case (yet common) scenario—a business that doesn't have a single client the first week it is open. The day you start your business, the countdown starts on draining your bank account. Knowing the amount you're starting with is critical.

Now, take the amount of money you've budgeted for your monthly expenses and add the amount of money that you've budgeted per month for marketing expenses. These are the two biggest things you'll need to worry about at first—your fixed expenses and your marketing budget. Fixed expenses are such expenses as rent (for both your personal and business spaces), insurance, licenses, and estimated self-employment taxes. Your marketing budget is the amount of money per month that you set aside to market your new business—something we'll talk about in great detail later. This amount of money should be set with online and print marketing in mind—and remember that online marketing can be free or very cheap. You'll also want to budget money for exhibiting at local wedding and event trade shows if you feel that doing so would be a good use of your time.

Aside from your fixed expenses, let's talk about when your business's first bills become due. Many small-business lenders have no problem extending out the date when a business's loans start becoming due, but you'll be paying way more interest in the long run. If the option presents itself, and resources allow, it's always better to start paying off your loans sooner. If your loans start becoming due right away, add them to your fixed expenses. If not, plan ahead for when they do.

At this point, you should be able to see how far your money is going to go, and that information should give you a good time frame for how fast you'll want to grow your business. If you're finding that your money won't last over six months, then you might have a problem. On average, it takes a business six to eight months to get a firm hold on its day-to-day operations—and that's not even factoring in if customers start coming or not. A lot of the necessary steps for success as a DJ will come well after you've opened your business (and, as we'll talk about in the next chapter, you'll most likely be overhauling a lot as time goes on).

Remember: Don't get in a rush. Success takes time, and the most successful DJs didn't become successes overnight. You're going to need to spend a lot of time marketing yourself, improving your efficiency as a DJ, and—the most time-consuming part—dealing directly with your clients, both new and old.

Who Needs a DJ?

As an aspiring DJ, you probably have an idea of exactly what kind of business you're looking to become. After all, there are a lot of types of DJ businesses out there—and many of them specialize in specific types of events. If you're like most DJs, regardless of your specific preferences in music, weddings will be the bread-and-butter of your business. Most weddings, in fact, hire DJs as their entertainment—and most weddings have a nice budget for entertainment. According to the American Disc Jockey Association, the average budget for a wedding DJ can be from $350 to $3,500—and according to entertainment booking powerhouse GigMasters, the average amount of money spent for entertainment at a wedding in the United States is $1,950. That's a lot of potential money for a small business to make on one gig!

Weddings may be the most profitable and steadiest type of work for you, but you should look out for a lot of other types of gigs to fill the gaps, especially in the winter when weddings are a slower market. Birthday parties, retirement parties, corporate events, and private entertainment venues are always on the lookout for entertainment, and DJs are at the top of the list. Being a great DJ is about a lot more than offering an impeccably thorough music collection and being able to make people dance; you'll also have to offer a superior value to your customers and to do whatever it takes to keep yourself competitive. It's a tough market out there—and the competition that can siphon off your customers' dollars should always be in the back of your head.

Beware of the (Diverse) Competition

Although DJs may be the most popular form of wedding entertainment, you're up against some other heavy-hitting, quickly growing forms of entertainment. According to GigMasters, one of the busiest entertainment booking companies in the industry, there's a trend toward hiring nonmusical entertainment—psychics, palm readers, and magicians being some of the fastest-growing forms—many of them creeping up on live music's number two spot (DJs maintain the number one position for wedding and private event markets).

First, keep an eye on your local economy and use that knowledge to your advantage. How's the local job market? Are people getting married and throwing receptions with the budgets they used to—remember that weddings will be your primary market—and are private events happening with any regularity and with budgets that include entertainment such as yourself? If you're in a smaller area where the economy has been poor and there's already some strong, well-respected competition, chances are you will find yourself with fewer clients.

While we're talking about building your client base in the face of stiff competition, let's talk about that local competition. The first step in determining how long it'll take for your DJ business to gain altitude is to evaluate your competition. We'll talk in more detail later about analyzing your competition, but as you're in the planning stages for your business, you need to keep in the back of your mind what you're up against. Even in a strong economy, how do you think you'll match up to what your competitors can offer from start to finish? Running a DJ business in an underserved area offers that population access to something that it normally would have to pay more to bring in from farther away. Unfortunately, some markets are simply too oversaturated to guarantee any type of immediate success. You'll have to work your way in and work hard to build your client base. If your local community has two or three strong competitors, it's going to take some work to knock them out of the saddle. Although I don't mean to make running a small business sound like competing in a medieval jousting match, in some ways it is.

I remember, years ago, my father planning a road trip for the family; I don't remember exactly where we were going, but in planning the route, he went to great lengths to map out exactly the course we'd take. He even went as far as going to the local library to pull out maps and atlases with much better detail than the one he had at home. Planning the route (and a contingency plan if things didn't work out) took days of research.

It may seem ridiculous in today's world of Google Maps and GPS navigation, but twenty years ago, that was the best way to find your route. Businesses are no different. And, unfortunately, running a business isn't nearly as easy as entering "an idea" as your starting point and "financial and personal success" as your destination in Google Maps. If it was, I wouldn't see small businesses closing every day. A business plan is still your best bet, and it's why we're dedicating a whole chapter to it.

Your business plan is, essentially, your roadmap to running a business. I won't say it's a roadmap to success—success is ultimately determined on how

Be Ready—and Flexible

Can you easily, in one sentence, define your business and its goals—and are you willing to modify that definition as time goes along? Don't laugh—many businesses have gone belly-up because they couldn't. You may find, at some point in your DJ business career, that you've got to change your focus to gain (or maintain) momentum. Be prepared!

well your business plan is executed and how well you roll with the punches of being a small business owner—but it's a great way to plot out your course.

A business plan, however, isn't the end-all and be-all of success. We'll talk more about that, too. In fact, a lot of business owners and consultants think that business plans aren't necessary at all (and that the concept is outdated in today's economy). I beg to differ. Although it's important to stay dynamic in your business's direction, you'll find that any successful business owner has a plan laid out—and financiers tend to like working with a business that has a plan.

I know—you probably want to dig more into the gritty details of being the best DJ you can be. However, if you're serious about this (and having bought this book shows that you are), you need to learn how to write a good, detailed business plan.

What a Business Plan Is—And Isn't

Let's get started on discussing your business plan, why you need it, and how you'll put it together. A business plan is, quite simply:

- a way to define your business
- an explanation of how you'll handle money (including funding, credit, and profits)
- a set of defined goals with an approximate time frame

A business plan is your best bet for starting a business in an organized, cohesive, and purpose-driven manner. However, it isn't an instant ticket to big-dollar financing and credit extensions. Some businesses are, surprisingly, able to draw up a single business plan and stick to it without faltering. That works in some businesses—but not all. You're thinking of starting a business in one of the most dramatically changing industries—the entertainment business—and one that will always require you to do some modification to your plan.

Most businesses will find that modifying their business plan as the days, weeks, months, and years go by is the best (and only) way to go, because businesses in today's economies have to be very dynamic to stay afloat. Yours will likely be no different.

What Makes a Good Business Plan?

Writing a business plan is an eye-opening experience. It's one that's surely caused a lot of bellyaching by potential new business owners, but it's one of the best ways to be prepared. After you've decided what your business is going to do and how you're

First, let's do an experiment to help you get started in the right direction when writing a business plan. We'll refer to these answers later—and then I'll show you what a completed business plan looks like. I'm going to give you a few blank lines to answer some questions right here in the book.

What do you want your DJ business to do?

_____

_____

_____

Do you know whom you plan to service with your business?

_____

_____

_____

How do you plan to finance opening a business?

_____

_____

_____

How will you define your success as a DJ business?

_____

_____

_____

How many competitors are in your area?

_____

_____

_____

What's going to make you unique?

_____

_____

_____

going to do it, getting those elements in writing is important. Business plans—especially the strict, no-deviation business plans of the past—aren't exactly necessary in today's economy, and some lenders won't even request them. But many will—and although businesspeople can debate the importance of a business plan until they're blue in the face, I—and many other small business operators—would be lost without one.

A good business plan is both dynamic and comprehensive. You'll need to be able to change your business's focus as times and circumstances change and especially if you need to change from full- to part-time. A great business plan will give you an overall picture of the health, outlook, and long-term goals for any small business while giving lots of flexibility to change as time goes on. That being said, let's look at what you'll need to be sure your business plan includes, even if the data within those sections change as your business evolves.

First, you should be able to describe accurately what your business does—and in this case, we know that you're going to be a DJ business that provides entertainment at events of all shapes, sizes, and budgets. Easy enough, right? Actually, you'll need to be more detailed and be prepared to discuss these aspects in remarkable detail with individuals who aren't familiar with your industry. Remember that a business plan isn't generally used as a peer-to-peer marketing tool. This document is most important to you for guidance, but it's equally important to others, mainly your partners, your investors, and your lenders. The people reading your business plan are going to be interested in seeing that you're well-spoken and that you avoid hyping your business beyond what the cold, hard facts show.

Next, you need to talk money. Business plans are generally most useful when you are obtaining credit and investments from others, and those people are always looking for the most accurate and in-depth picture of your financial situation. They want to know how your financial planning is going, and they want to know how prepared you are for the time period before you start making a profit. Being able to tell your potential investors exactly what you'll do to make money with your DJ business, how you'll spend that money, and how you'll invest that money back into your business is important. They're going to want to know how your business will be paying back any monies paid out to you and if you'll be able to afford the interest and payments. You won't be expected to show them easy riches—we know that your business will be unlikely to make you a millionaire in the next couple of years—but lenders do need to see that you've got a positive outlook. Even if you anticipate just barely meeting your break-even point or posting a small loss after expenses, readers of your business plan deserve your honesty.

Now, let's look at constructing that business plan yourself.

The Executive Summary

The first part of any successful business plan is the executive summary, which describes you and your business. This isn't a place to hype the fact that you're the latest and greatest DJ in all the land—and it's not a place to brag about things that aren't directly related to the operation of your business. To a lender or investor, a good business doesn't need self-generated hype. All you need is a good, firm grip on what your business will do. It doesn't matter how great you think your business's plans may be. What matters most to an investor is that the business stands out on its own, fills a void in a profitable market, and can generate income by tapping into as many markets as possible.

In your executive summary, you should start by introducing your business as well as your business plan itself. Let the reader know what a DJ business does—plainly, without use of technical jargon and hip, industry lingo. This isn't a place to talk about "hitting the decks" and making "fat beats"—you're not selling to an industry peer. I know that explaining something to a nontechnical, nonmusical individual can be a daunting task for some—myself included—because it's always safe to fall back into what's familiar and comfortable for you. But being able to explain your business calmly and thoroughly is the first step in writing a good executive summary. In describing your business, you should explain who your customers are, where they're located, and how you'll reach them. It's equally important to introduce your business plan's goal. If you're actively shopping for funding, credit lines, endorsements, or sponsorships, let your readers know. They should be able to find out, within the first few paragraphs of your executive summary, who you are and why you're talking to them.

At this point, you should also explain where your business will do things differently to set it apart from the competition. You should have, by this point, researched your competition to find out what you're up against. If twenty other DJs in town are doing exactly what you want to do, that's probably a good indication that you need to hone in on a specific, specialized market when it comes to advertising.

Business Summary and Description—The Finer Details

After you've described the basics of who you are, what your business is, and how you'll pull it off, it's time to explain your business in greater detail. This isn't where you detail the process of being a DJ. This is where you describe how your business will be structured—first in summary and then in fine detail. You need to be able to discuss whether the business is going to be a sole proprietorship, a partnership, or a corporation (more on this in chapter 6). You also need to describe your place of business, how you're prepared to be a running DJ operation, and how you'll pay for the costs related to opening the doors. Remember that you're going after potential partners and investors here—you'll need to show them that your business has a spine before they jump onboard.

A good business description generally covers the first year of your operations. You'll need to let your readers know how much money you're investing to get off the ground and how much you'll need to funnel into the business to keep it operating through its first year—generally the hardest time for small businesses. And readers want to hear about a lot before you even open the doors: They want to know, in detail, why you need their investment and what of your own you've put into it. They want details on the logistics of operating your business, what kind of space you'll operate from, and how you'll handle legal and financial conflict.

Being able to describe the legal standing of your business is an important element—and one you'll need to sort out right away. Most self-employed people are considered sole proprietors, but many choose to form corporations, either traditional or limited liability. If two people are working together, you'll be considered a partnership unless you choose to incorporate in some way.

Now that your business is described in generalities, it's time to dig deeper into the operations of your business.

Here comes the easiest part of your business plan: describing in fine detail what you plan to do, day in and day out. Keep in mind that not all of the readers of your business plan have a reason to learn the day-to-day plan for your business; they're interested only in how much money you plan to make and how carefully you'll manage yourself against the competition. That being said, many people who read your business plan will want a picture of how your business's overall operations are run, and they need to be able to walk away with a decent understanding of what a DJ business does, even if you've got to go way out of your way to simplify the information so that somebody who isn't as hip in the ways of the DJ business can make sense of it all.

Here's your time to shine. If there's one thing you know best, it's being a DJ—and you know that you're good enough to be starting a business in the first place. Now's the time to go into great detail and show just how much you really know (and how prepared you are).

In coming up with your business description, you should be able to answer, in detail, some important questions:

- What does a good DJ business do for its customers?
- How do you retain (and keep happy) your clientele?
- What's your customer service policy?
- How will you ensure repeat business?
- How do you make sure that your DJ business stands out against the well-seated competition?

Market Analysis

Now that you've figured out the purpose and basic structure of your business, we're going to have to size up your local competition. Knowing the competition and understanding how it wins over customers are important for any new business. Although most small businesses tend to take a friendly attitude to each other—there's a certain "we're in this together" attitude among many small business owners—this is still a business, and you've got a bottom line to look after; gathering as much intelligence on your competition as you can is vital to making sure you earn as many customers as you can before the competition has a shot at them.

After you've figured out the necessary data—use the "DJ Market Evaluation" worksheet on page 23 to help you—these should be packaged and presented as part of your overall business plan. Investors and partners will want to know your realistic chances of taking a worthwhile chunk of your competition's business. Maybe your market is too small for two DJ services—that's something you might learn in this stage of your business (although I hope that's not the case). Maybe your market is saturated with DJ services, but they're missing a major niche market that could easily sustain your small operation. That's what market research data do for you; there's a reason why large corporations spend millions of dollars a year to better understand their competition's products and services.

In this section, you'll also describe the buyer market for your services. As we know, weddings are the number one source of work for DJs—and good wedding DJs have bookings months in advance (complete with cash deposits) and make a great living by working a few nights a week. You should be able to describe the wedding market in great detail—and you should have a good idea of where else your services are needed.

As I'm sure you've figured out by now, the DJ business as a whole is a remarkably successful, wildly in-demand segment of the entertainment industry. That being said, a lot of people out there are trying to do exactly what you're doing. As you know, being a good DJ is about consistency, variety, and ability to adapt to a wide range of situations, even before you look at the overwhelming amount of business planning that goes into running a successful enterprise, regardless of what you're offering. It's important to know where you stand against your competitors. Knowing everything you can about your competition is the best way to go head-to-head. It'll also help you identify markets that are traditionally underserved by DJs in your area—maybe certain ethnic or religious groups prefer certain specialties in entertainment, and you may be at an advantage if you can offer them.

When sizing up your competition—and your market—you should keep in mind a few important questions when writing your business plan:

How many competitors are in your area?

_____

In your area, what's the average price of a wedding DJ for a standard reception? This price should give your business plan's reader a good idea of how much your standard wedding gig will net.

_____

How much do corporate events tend to pay?

_____

How many large corporations are located in your area? Large corporations spend a lot, even in today's economy, on entertainment for their employee events.

_____

What's the average income in your area? Providing higher-end services to the wedding and celebration market in an area with lots of wealth is a no-brainer, but there's no problem at all if your market supports more modestly priced services.

_____

Breaking Even

Being in business for yourself is a challenge, and it can be an overwhelmingly confusing endeavor when it comes to managing money. Money is a tricky element for small businesses, especially sole proprietorships; you've got to carefully manage your business's financial health, which is directly tied in to your personal finances.

For most business plans, any investor or partner who reads your plan will be looking for something called a _break-even point_. The break-even point is the amount of money you need to have coming in every month to cover your operating expenses. Remember that evaluation we did earlier about being able to define your business's timeline by watching the amount of money you have to spend? You'll need to tell the reader of your business plan how much you need to meet your expenses. You'll also need to describe, plain and simply, how your business will make money. That means explaining how your pricing structure will work, what your average client is anticipated to spend, and how you came up with the amount you charge. Readers don't want to deal with somebody who prices his or her products without some sort of master plan—without that specific detail, it's hard to figure out sales goals.

In finding your break-even point (and how you'll achieve it), ask yourself the following questions:

- What's the cost to run your business monthly? We figured this out earlier.
- How much money does an average DJ client spend on services?
- Does the amount you charge depend on the event?
- How do you handle overtime?
- How many gigs, at your average rate, do you need per month to break even?

After you've determined how much you need and how you can theoretically achieve it, your business plan readers will feel a whole lot better about lending you money or partnering with your business. They want to see that you've got a grip on the financial realities of running a small business—and they want to see that you understand that some months can be a close call when it comes to making ends meet. But that thorough understanding, even if the outcome looks bleak at first, shows that you know your stuff, even when you're not behind the mic.

Sample Business Plan

A business plan isn't easy to write. It's a lot to remember and a lot to explain—and I know from personal experience that the process of explaining what you do to people who aren't as passionate about the business's activities as they are about the business's financial picture can be frustrating. Remember, though, that all businesses, large or small, need some level of organization to be successful. Starting with a thorough business plan is the best way to give yourself a roadmap, even if you have to constantly update your goals, procedures, and target market.

Take a look at a real business plan included on pages 25–28 for a DJ business just like yours. Although this business plan is comprehensive for the business it was written for, it may not suit yours individually. Remember that all businesses are different—and there's no single roadmap to success for any of them.

DJ Services, LLC

A New York Limited Liability Company

Business Plan

1. Executive Summary

The purpose of this business plan is to offer a roadmap to the successful operation of DJ Services, LLC, a proposed mobile DJ service located in the New York City area. DJ Services, LLC will tentatively begin operations on November 10, 2011. Jack Green is a professional DJ, having worked for four years as a wedding DJ for Master DJ Service of Brooklyn.

What follows is a brief summary of the information contained within this business plan, as applies to DJ Services, LLC.

A.) DJ Services, LLC plans to open for public business on November 10, 2011.

B.) The sole purpose of DJ Services, LLC will be to offer affordable, high-quality DJ services for clients of all varieties, with a special eye toward the wedding market. In the New York City area, the average wedding spends over $1,900 on entertainment alone.

C.) Initially, the business will offer services on a part-time, as-needed basis. As the business grows, Mr. Green plans to go full-time with his venture.

D.) The business also plans to distinguish itself from existing competition by use of high-quality, portable sound reinforcement, with an eye toward being modular for expansion in the future. Clients can expect technological innovations to be a forefront focus of the business, allowing better quality and more efficient production. This includes use of high-quality digital storage (offering unprecedented selection and variety for any event, thanks to the ultra-low cost of data storage).

DJ Services, LLC and proprietor Jack Green are tremendously confident in the business's ability to attract and retain a quality paying customer base. This plan intends to serve as a one-stop guide to all activities leading up to and within the everyday operations of the business and will allow management of the business to have a firm hold on the direction the business must take in order to remain profitable for not only itself but also the lenders and partners who trust their name to the business.

2. Business Summary

DJ Services, LLC will open in November, 2011. This business will be managed by Jack Green and will be legally structured as a limited liability corporation. Jack Green is currently the sole financial investor of the project and anticipates investing $24,000 of his own money into the business. This $24,000 is currently in an interest-bearing savings account and is considered "cash on hand." Aside from this initial self-invested seed money, Jack Green estimates that he will need an additional $20,000 for equipment and business expenses. Mr. Green plans to acquire this through partnering with low-interest business lenders.

DJ Services, LLC will be established as an "at-home" business, with equipment being stored onsite in Mr. Green's garage. Clerical space will be inside, in a 400-square-foot office space in a spare bedroom. This will cut down on the overhead of the business because it will be included in the monthly mortgage payment that Jack Green is already paying. This monthly mortgage expense will become a burden of the business, for the purposes of maintaining a quality location to operate from without incurring additional undue expenses.

DJ Services, LLC plans to utilize exceptionally advanced live sound reinforcement equipment to offer an exceedingly satisfactory client experience. As such, equipment purchasing encompasses the bulk of start-up spending for most DJ setups.

- Approximately $39,000 will be used for equipment purchases.

- $2,000 will be earmarked for office-related expenses.

- Another $2,000 will operate as an emergency fund. This is money the business owner plans to keep in an interest-bearing savings account the duration of the life of the $20,000 loan. This will be used as emergency cash for equipment repairs or issues that may arise. If this money remains untouched to the end of the loan—and the business continues operating in a positive cash-flow environment—the $2,000 will act as the final payment on the loan. This assures the business will remain free of debilitating revolving debt in case of hard times.

- $1,000 will be used strictly for marketing purposes within the first six months of operation. Athough this number is low by industry standards, the business plans to advertise in prepicked locations where the target market will be reached most often and with more positive impressions than anywhere else.

This money is earmarked as follows:

- $500 for an Internet presence design, including a small website, business card and logo design, and online portfolio design;

- $100 for monthly hosting fees, paid on a biannual basis;

- $400 to be used for pay-as-you-go Internet advertising, paid classified ads, and small print ads.

Day-to-day, nonperformance operations at DJ Services, LLC will consist of contacting prospective clients, offering a description of services, maintaining live performance equipment, obtaining and updating musical libraries, and working on scheduling.

3. Market Analysis

The target market for DJ Services, LLC is, primarily, weddings. Weddings make up the bulk of any DJ business, with, according to independent research, 85 percent of weddings choosing a DJ over other forms of entertainment. The secondary market will be generally described as "private and corporate" events. At this time, DJ Services, LLC does not plan to expand into the nightclub market, although plans for future expansion always remain dynamic.

Competition is fairly steep. Within a 10-mile radius, there are fifteen other registered DJ businesses. Some of those DJ services cater to specific demographics—the Jewish wedding circuit being one of the largest specialty markets, which services both weddings and religious services.

Depending on the service rendered, the competition's researched pricing averages between $500 and $3,500. An average spend for a small to medium-sized wedding is $1,500. Billing of events will be done on a sliding-scale basis, charging clients based on actual time performed, travel distance, and logistical challenges. Understanding the market and how to meet its needs will be one of the cornerstones of DJ Services, LLC. As such, DJ Services, LLC will spend an initial budget of $1,000 on marketing, which will include sponsorship of local non-profit events, a web and social networking presence, and free download of mix tapes and performance examples for prospective clients.

In summary:

- DJ Services, LLC's primary target market is the ever-in-demand wedding market.

- The most common target demographic is couples being married for the first time, with an average age range of twenty-five to thirty-five.

- The secondary market for DJ Services, LLC will be private event clients, both corporate and institutional. Schools and colleges, of which there are numerous examples in the area, regularly utilize DJ services to provide entertainment.

4. Break-Even Estimates

Monthly, the business will start operations with a deficit of $1,250. This includes the cost of rent ($700), the projected loan payment of $300 ($20,000 at a reasonable percentage rate, approximately $300 per month), and $250 earmarked for business expenses, including additional utilities and supplies such as paper, ink, replacement parts, and servicing.

- Monthly deficit: $1,250

- Hourly rate, average wedding client (average ticket of eight hours divided by $1,500, average single-event price): $187.50

- Monthly break-even point: $1,250

5. Conclusion

DJ Services, LLC feels quite ready to establish itself as a market leader in the New York City metro area. With a combination of high-tech sound reinforcement equipment and excellent customer service, DJ Services, LCC is poised to be a market leader in the region.

This combination of fair pricing and expert knowledge will combine to create a business with large potential profit per month. In fact, one week's profit could potentially reach $1,400—assuming all billable hours in one week are reserved by clients.

With a relatively low debt and very few expenses, DJ Services, LLC will be able to easily turn a profit, if business can be grown at a steady pace. DJ services are plentiful in the area, but none offers the amenities and quality service that DJ Services, LLC will offer. With a commitment to being the best recording provider in the New York metro area, DJ Services, LLC has the potential to become a major player—and thus expand greatly in both clientele and studio quality.

By now you've probably had some time to work on your business plan and you're ready to start the hard work of establishing your DJ business. Now, let's talk about exactly what you'll need to turn your passion for DJing into a successful business. As we're getting into these more advanced topics, I'll assume that you're a DJ who knows the basics of spinning and emceeing—we'll talk more about larger-scale sound reinforcement, professional-grade equipment, and other more advanced tricks of the trade later—and that you've charted a course for your aspiring DJ business throughout your business plan. That's great—you'll need that information as we go along.

Remember that you're bound to find things about your business plan that you want to change as we go along, and that's totally fine. Make those changes and follow your gut instinct when you feel you're going down the wrong path in some area. There's no shame in modifying your business to better meet the needs of your local clientele after you've started to get all kinds of clients, either. After all, they're the ones who keep you in business.

Choosing a Name

This is one of the most fun parts of starting your own business—choosing a name that you want your business to be known by. I'm sure you've already done this, but in case you haven't, I doubt you'll have to look far for inspiration. After you've selected a name, you need to research your competition. You don't want a name that sounds too close to that of a well-established competitor, and you want your name to stand out in your market. Being unique is always a plus, but make sure you appear professional with the name you've selected.

You should also be careful about deliberate misspellings in your business name. Although the practice has roots in old trademark law (trademarking generic combinations of words can cause quite the headache for business owners), deliberate misspellings somehow became a way to express creativity when starting a business. Although it might be tempting to call your business "PhatJamz, Inc.," you need to remember to whom you're selling. Chances are your clients will appreciate a much more professional company appearance—even if they expect you to be an energetic emcee and motivate everybody to get on the dance floor come event time.

After you've selected a name, it's time to register it—and trademark it.

Don't Lose Your Own Name!

Choosing a name is important for another reason: As a growing business, you want a good chance to cement your place in your market. You don't need somebody using your name after you're successful, and you certainly don't need somebody trying to edge you out by using your business name after you've become successful because he or she laid claim to it properly before you did.

Registering Your Business

The first, easiest, and most inexpensive way to make your business official is to register an employer identification number (EIN) under your business's name. Although you still need to take action to preserve your right to use your business name, registering an EIN notifies the government, by way of the IRS, that you're conducting business under this name. An EIN is the number that you'll use when establishing business credit, paying taxes, and reporting wages paid. After you've got an EIN, you're able to have a number similar to a Social Security number that is independently verifiable as belonging to your business. Obtaining an EIN is free and requires nothing more than filling out a simple online form. You'll need to know what legal structure you plan to use for your business as well.

Don't be fooled by online ads—a lot of companies promise to register an EIN for you quickly for a fee. This service isn't necessary (and borders on illegal): Going to the IRS's website, www.irs.gov, and searching for "EIN Application" will bring you to the quick and free official application. You'll have your new EIN in minutes.

If you're going to operate as most self-employed people do, you'll register as a sole proprietor or as part of a partnership. In this case, you'll need to register what's known as a *fictitious name* or *doing business as (dba)* with your state (again, more on this in chapter 6). This process is also usually painless and quick and doesn't require a large payment. This process officially registers the business name as belonging to you and as being used to do business in the state. The process varies among states, so there's no way I can list the variations here; refer to your secretary of state's website for more information on exactly what you need to do.

However, if you're going the more complicated route of becoming a limited liability corporation (LLC) or corporation, you won't need to register a dba or fictitious name; when your state's paperwork for incorporation is filed, the filing automatically registers the business name with the state much in the same way.

Trademarking Your Brand

Next, you should look into trademarking your name—and your company's logo, if you have one.

Registering your trademark gives you exclusive use of your business's name, likeness, and any other traits that you wish to make note of to set yourself apart from your competition. Registering a trademark is a much more complicated process than registering an EIN or a dba; you might find that you're confused and need to consult an attorney with practice in trademarks and copyright. That's an expensive path to take, but it's not uncommon to need this help.

First, you have to determine if your preferred business trademark is already being used by somebody else—or if there's a very similar trademark that might cause a conflict later. Remember, when it comes to intellectual property, that it's always way cheaper and much wiser to avoid problems at the beginning rather than to think you can sort them out in court later. It's easy and free to search trademarks; just go to www.uspto.gov.

After you've verified that the name you want is up for grabs, you need to file for the trademark protection itself. On the same government website, you can fill out the form to make the trademark official as well as pay the $325 fee (the current amount at this time). You also must include an example that shows the government exactly what you want protected—be it a business name, logo, or other proprietary design unique to your business. In your case, you'll just need to register the name of your DJ business and maybe a logo if you have one.

Now, you wait patiently. A response can take six to eight months, and that response might be "no." The government can reject trademarks for a variety of reasons, some of which may be obscure and not directly apply to your case, but the government will still stick hard to the rules. If you're approved, you don't have anything else to do. Your registration is good for ten whole years.

Setting Up Your HQ

Before you do anything else, you should consider registering a business phone number for your business. This number can be for a phone on a land line (preferably one that can forward to a cell phone), an Internet-based service (MagicJack and Vonage are popular choices), or a cellular provider. Although it may seem redundant, doing this helps prove that—even if you're operating from your home—you're a serious business with a real, physical presence. Many financial institutions and credit companies won't open accounts without it.

After your phone number is registered, you'll need to do whatever you can to get that number—and the name of your business—listed in directory services everywhere possible. It's important that your customers be able to find you, but there's another important reason that not many business owners realize: One of the most common methods that credit processors use to verify a legitimate business is to call directory assistance and ask for a number—and then verify that the number is a commercial line. Your being listed in every directory possible makes it easier for these companies to verify your business as legitimate.

Your Website

I remember that when I started my first business, websites were relatively new. It was still necessary to hit the pavement, advertising by hand (and placing flyers on cars—something I don't miss doing). How times have changed! Now, if you don't have a website proudly advertising your business, you're far behind the times.

Establishing your presence on the web isn't necessarily expensive, but it's time-consuming to do yourself and requires a certain level of familiarity with html, graphic design, and the web-hosting process. Still, the stigma of not having a solid web presence is enough to turn off many potential customers; think about it: If you look up a restaurant and can't find an active website with hours and a recent menu, you're going to think twice about eating there, right?

Building a website on a budget doesn't have to be problematic. Many hosting services will give you a break on hosting fees if you purchase six months or more of hosting time; this option can bring your monthly cost down to $5 or less. And design is cheap, too—many designers will make a simple, functional website for under $100. It's not important to be fancy, just thorough.

When building your website, you should ask yourself a few questions:

- *What do you want to showcase?* Make sure you're showing off your equipment, any sound or video clips, your song list, and customer testimonials.
- *How are your design skills?* If you're not confident that you can make something that stands out, don't waste your time doing it yourself. Make sure you hire a professional to save yourself time and embarrassment.
- *Make sure your diversity shows.* As we'll talk about later, you'll need to serve a wide range of ethnic and religious clientele. Show that you understand the local markets.

Banking and Credit—The Baby Steps

Later, we'll talk about how to establish business credit and how to properly pay your taxes while reporting your earnings to the government. Business credit is absolutely essential for some businesses, but yours may operate well without it. It just depends on what you're bringing to the table in the beginning and on what you've got coming in down the road. For now, we need to work on establishing a financial presence for your business.

In the last few years, obtaining business credit has been difficult for small businesses. The rate of businesses folding and leaving lenders without a way to recoup their losses has been incredibly high. Establishing a thorough picture of your business's financial health is absolutely essential for being able to get and maintain business credit.

First, you need to establish a business checking account. After you've become a legal business in the eyes of the federal government (more on this later), you'll qualify to open a commercial checking account at a banking institution of your choice. Business checking generally requires that you present proof of business, including an EIN and local business license. You'll also need to give your own Social Security number, and the bank will generally run a check on ChexSystems or Tele-Check to verify that you're in good standing at other financial institutions. If you're not, chances are the bank won't approve you.

After you've gotten your account, it's time to put money into it—and leave it there. Maintaining a high minimum balance in the first few months of your business is crucial to forming business credit because banks will generally check banking references, and they like to see a well-maintained positive balance. It's also important because often a bank will offer lines of credit based on the overall balance you normally carry. Establishing this balance—even if it's only a couple of thousand dollars—is important at this stage in the game.

Online Client Payment

How often are you frustrated because you can't pay a bill online? I know I get easily frustrated—if it weren't for online bill pay, I wouldn't be up-to-date on as many accounts as I am. Being able to let your clients pay online is important in today's digital world. As you slowly get yourself established in the financial sector of your business planning, you'll want to look into taking online client payments. Being able to take online quickly and easily is one of the hallmarks of a modern business.

Many small businesses accept credit cards. Being able to accept credit cards directly on your website isn't necessary, but it's a great way for your clients to pay their deposits and service fees. Setting up merchant services via your website provider is generally easy and doesn't cost much money. Clients will be able to use their credit cards directly on your website, attached to your merchant account you set up with the credit card companies.

Aside from direct payment on your website, a variety of sites facilitates online payment without a merchant account. PayPal is one of the best, and it's the most popular online payment service for auctions and person-to-person transactions. Its business services division is very robust and easy to work with, and all you'll need is your business name and EIN to get started. You can then take online credit card and check payments from your customers with zero liability for fraud. However you choose to accept online payment, being prepared for customers who, like myself, prefer to pay everything without speaking to another person is a great way to make sure you have all of your bases covered.

Taking online payment isn't without risk. You're still putting yourself in a position where your client may turn over data that are stolen or misused by someone hacking the processing company or sniffing out the secure transaction. These types of events are getting more and more rare—and when they happen, it's usually because people used a credit card on the Internet somewhere they shouldn't have.

Now that you've established your business bank accounts, your EIN, and all of your paperwork in order with the government, it's time to dig deeper. Let's look at some specific issues in the DJ business and at ways by which you can start your business out by being—from the beginning—the consummate professional DJ. Here's where the fun stuff starts.

05 From the Ground Up—Marketing

Now that you've taken the time to write out a business plan and figure out how you're going to start your business, it's time to get started with the stuff you came here to do: start a DJ business. This is where the fun stuff starts—but even though you've got the foundation of your business set in stone, there's still a lot of work to get done. In today's high-tech and fast-moving world of Internet advertising and social media, opening the doors to your business and placing an ad in the local newspaper aren't enough (and, in fact, putting an ad in your local paper may be the biggest waste of money ever). Marketing, in today's world, isn't usually the most expensive part of running a business—at least it doesn't have to be!

When you think of marketing, you need to think like the people you're planning on serving. What appeals to them? What makes them confident in the decision to hire you for your services? It's something that takes a lot of guesswork.

Starting a business can be stressful, as I'm sure you've figured out by now. In later chapters, we'll talk in-depth about how to run your DJ business as a whole and how to be a more consummate DJ professional: how to select songs, how to market to different demographics, and how to have the best sound system possible for a variety of situations. For now, we've got some more behind-the-scenes work to get done—keep in mind that you're still the new kid on the block. Even with a great business plan and killer DJ skills, you need to find a way to rope in your clients.

So, let's look at where we are. We've envisioned your business and planned what you're going to do, and now it's time to start marketing your business to the public. You've got a great product, you're confident in your skills, and all that's missing are your customers—so let's go get them.

Whom Do You Serve?

Now that you've gotten yourself on the right path to starting your DJ business, it's time to ask yourself a few questions about starting your marketing efforts. You know that your business is special—so it's time to share that knowledge with the world.

Your customers, as any business owner knows, are the most important thing any business has. Without customers, a business fails. A business cannot stay afloat if people don't use its services or products. Making any business work is about finding the people who most need your products and finding every way under the sun to convince them to hire you. From there, it's about word-of-mouth promotion. It goes without saying that every gig you do as a new DJ isn't about just the money—it's also about advertising. You're a walking advertisement for yourself.

Let's think about who needs your services. Your primary market should be, as any professional DJ will tell you, **weddings**. Wedding receptions will likely be your most common source of business, and the more types of people you're able to provide services for, the more business you'll get. Weddings are also generally high-paying gigs due to the high demand—many weddings budget thousands of dollars on entertainment. And the more professional is the package you can offer for a reasonable price, the more business you'll have. In chapter 12, we'll examine the wedding market in detail.

Targeting New Clientele

So, whom can you serve as a DJ business? A lot of entertainment money is up for grabs, and if you know where to look, you can go after as much business as you can responsibly handle. Here are some of the common—and not-so-common—events and clients you might be able to pursue in your local market:

- Weddings (obviously). But also parties leading up to weddings such as engagement parties, rehearsal dinners, etc.
- Bar/bat mitzvahs
- Christenings/baptisms
- Sweet sixteen parties
- Adult birthday parties
- Theme parties (decades, musical styles, etc.)
- Fundraisers
- Skate parties
- Sports teams/pep rallies
- Private schools (dances, graduations)
- Ethnic celebrations
- Carnivals
- Corporate events
- Government clients (armed forces, correctional institutions, state schools)

Private events are your second-biggest target market. Private events are just about everything else except weddings: birthday parties, christenings, bar/bat mitzvahs, retirement parties—the list goes on and on. Fortunately for you, private events are as varied as the people who'll be holding them—which means a lot of potential business. Any event where there are people who need entertainment means a potential client for you. It's up to you to find them.

I know that sounds vague, and it might feel like I'm not guiding you in the right direction, but here's one thing to remember from one business owner to another: You're lucky in your decision to open a DJ business. Unlike some businesses, you're in a position to truly service a large segment of the population, depending on how far you decide to reach to meet new clients. The more versatile your DJ business is, the more clients you can attract. Parties, family gatherings, and weddings are all as diverse as the people attending, and being able to serve many demographics can only help.

DJ versus Band

Live music has become increasingly popular—and potentially profitable. In today's independent music scene, thousands of talented bands are playing in venues everywhere—many making absolutely nothing after a night's gig. Unfortunately, that means that many musicians are extra hungry to make a buck on the side—and that creates your number one competition. Live bands have historically taken a back seat to DJs, especially in recent years. In fact, according to a poll conducted by *St. Louis Bride & Groom Magazine,* 65 percent of couples who hired live musicians regretted their decision and wished they had hired a DJ service instead. That's an overwhelming number of disappointed customers. Even with those types of statistics against them, bands are still your most likely competition.

Although live music can be a fun way to provide entertainment for an event, it can get costly quickly. That's one area where you as a DJ have live music beat. Any professional-quality band, even one made up of local musicians, will generally try to pay members at least $200 per wedding or private gig—and often more. Paying four or more band members and paying the fees for moving equipment and renting a sufficient sound system, staging, lighting, and all the other elements that come with a band performance—whether the cost is packaged through the band or contracted by the buyer—are expensive. To do it all on the cheap usually means hiring a low-quality, pro-amateur band that's best suited for playing the local drinking hall.

Variety is another area where you have most bands beat. At weddings, the bride and groom may have thirty songs between them that they want played—songs from their dating years, songs from their college days, and whatever else they think will be fun to dance to with their friends. A bride may request jazz during dinner and rockabilly all night long—and only you can provide that. Generally, bands hired for weddings are either cover bands (bands whose repertoire consists of only well-known songs) or tribute bands (bands whose repertoire consists of songs of one particular artist with a stage show exhibiting some traits of the original artist). Few weddings hire original bands, even though original bands tend to charge a lower fee due to lower demand. Original bands, especially mid-level and top-name artists, are frequently hired for private and corporate events—but the events they're brought in for probably wouldn't be appropriate for a DJ in the first place.

If you've got a potential client who's trying to decide between live music and your DJ services, here are three big selling points, in summary, that you can use to persuade that person to hire you:

1. **Bands have more people to pay.** Depending on how many members a band has plus road crew and booking agent commissions, there are a lot of hands in the pot—and a lot of ways to drive up the cost, with sound, lighting, and staging generally being the most expensive. DJs typically are single-person operations, and that keeps costs down.

2. **DJs offer more variety.** Remind your client that only DJs can carry thousands of songs in their back pocket—and that any DJ worth his or her fee can make absolutely anything happen. Bands are limited to the repertoire they've rehearsed.

3. **DJs let the hosts—and the party itself—be the star of the show unless otherwise asked.** Bands offer a stage show that makes them the center of attention. As a DJ, you can and should take the mic and show off your emcee skills when appropriate and requested but still keep the party itself the center of attention.

Your Demo

Later, we'll talk about fine-tuning the song list that you use for your DJ performances. Creating your song list is an absolutely mammoth undertaking—one of the hardest things you tackle on your road to becoming a successful DJ, and we'll spend an entire chapter later on getting it right. It's one area of maintenance that you'll need to stay on top of. As a DJ service, you need to offer an extremely wide variety of music to make people happy, and you need to spend a lot of time making sure that collection is up-to-date with the latest hits (and classics). For now, let's talk about your demo.

Just like a band seeking to get booked for a venue or event, you'll need demos that showcase your best work for a variety of clients.

Making a demo doesn't have to be a hard process, but it will take some work. In order to do it properly, you'll need to have a basic understanding of audio file editing—something that you may or may not be prepared to do. Audio editing is a necessary skill, and you'll eventually want to be able to make mash-ups and custom-edited songs. Even basic audio editing can come in handy—and give you an extra service that you can offer your clients—for extra pay, of course!

Many DJs do produce video demos. A demo is a great way to show you using your emcee skills along with the guests at your events enjoying themselves. A good video demo should show that you're able to work a crowd, deal well with special requests, and stop at nothing to offer a fun, exciting, and professional experience from set-up to tear-down. Potential clients also want to see your behind-the-scenes activities and to what lengths you go to make your clients happy.

If you're not able to produce a good video demo, then it's generally a good idea to hire a professional who can help you. A bad video demo isn't useful; it's better to not do a video demo until you can afford to do one properly.

If you decide to go the video demo route, keep in mind two key points:

1. **Appear professional.** Although it might be tempting to showcase your business in a *The Office*-style mockumentary, the humor might be lost on potential clients who expect a professional for their $130-per-plate dinner reception. You want to appeal to clients of all varieties—high-dollar and budget. Being professional, honest, and thorough with your descriptions of your business and how you showcase yourself will go a long way.

2. **Never compromise on sound.** Even in today's world of cheap HD cameras and easy editing software such as iMovie, most amateur video productions appear, well, amateur. Why? The audio quality is poor. Just plain bad. Make sure that you—or whoever is producing your video—take the time to do the sound properly. That means using lavaliere microphones (small microphones inconspicuously attached to your person) to capture up-close speech, shotgun microphones (longer microphones with a highly directional scope) for far-away voice and ambience, and direct feeds from your microphone and mixer—called *soundboard recordings*—to bring a high-quality touch to your program material. It's much more professional, especially as a DJ, to have your work showcased in the best sound quality possible.

Also, make sure that any event or person you film signs an appearance release form. You'll need to do this at any show that you plan to videotape for promotional purposes because anybody who appears in the video must consent to it. Any people who don't consent to it could theoretically sue you if they don't like how they're portrayed in your video. A quick, easy release form can be written by anybody—just state the person's name and the fact that the person agrees to appear in your video for noncommercial reasons. You're not making a profit off of the person; he or she is simply participating in a demonstration video that you need to show to potential clients. Chances are that such people will absolutely love showing off how perfect their event was.

To produce a great audio demo, you've got to hone those audio editing skills we talked about earlier—or hire a professional to do the demo for you. It's easy to put a bunch of songs on a CD or MP3 mix and call it a mix representative of your tastes, but that doesn't give the potential client more than a very narrow perspective of what you can do. You'll want to give the listener a chronological experience of an average event—and because most of your events will be weddings, it's wise to spend the most time and effort producing a demo that directly markets itself to wedding clients.

Sample Demo Elements

Before building your demo, let's take a look at what should go into your demo. This isn't a hard-and-fast rule, but it's certainly good advice: Showcase your services as an emcee first and then show your client how you'd respond, as a DJ, to a variety of requests.

I tend to recommend that demos showcase several elements:

- *An introduction.* Introduce yourself and your DJ business. Make this brief. Let listeners know that you're going to walk them through and let them know how they can contact you.

- *A sample wedding introduction.* This can be recorded from a real gig or produced in your office. You want to show a couple what a real wedding introduction can be like—and how well your personality as a DJ comes through. Remember that they're going to want you to appear professional. Make sure you show that you have a variety of choices of entrance songs as well. Many couples will choose their own, but you've got to be prepared to offer selections for those who want one but are unable to tell you something they have in mind.

- *Samples of dinner music and cocktail-hour music, with announcements.* Your potential clients will be looking for versatility, and that will most likely include music for before the real party begins. Include some sample announcements—let the guests know that dinner will be served soon, that the bar is open, and any other announcements you think might be necessary at this point. On this playlist, they'll want to hear jazz, blues, folk, and acoustic music. Remember, too, that many weddings hire live music for pre-dance slots—that's another chance for you to lose money. Showing that you can handle both tasks elegantly is important.

- *Sample pop/Top 40 playlist.* This is the part of your demo that will require updating frequently. Show that you understand what good pop music is— and that you've got all the latest hits. Showcase remixes, mash-ups, and everything that's current in the pop scene. You'll get asked to play a variety of these songs for most events.

- *First dance songs.* Show that you have an understanding of how the "first dance" tradition works. You might also include announcements relevant to this.

- *Parent dances.* The dances for the bride and her father and for the groom and his mother are another popular tradition at many weddings. A lot of songs can fit this bill, and your potential client will want to see that you know a lot of them. Showcase both types of dances and the appropriate announcements.
- *Group dances.* Show your skills in rounding up people on the dance floor to participate in group activities. Line dances—however out of style—continue to be a fun tradition shared at many weddings. Show that you know how to emcee people onto the dance floor and show an understanding of many of the most popular group dances, past and present.
- *Diversity.* Show that you can cater to groups of ethnic and religious backgrounds. More on this specifically later, but showing that you can play a selection of music for all demographics is important.
- *Rock and roll—all kinds of it.* Show that you can play soft rock, hard rock, metal, blues rock, and just about every other kind of music recorded by a band with lots of electric guitars. Showcase rock hits and indie-rock cult classics. Show an understanding and respect for both old and new.
- *Hip hop/R&B.* Show an understanding of what's late and great in the hip-hop and R&B worlds. Slow songs, upbeat jams, and pop-rap are all popular at weddings, even with an otherwise diverse taste in the rest of the music.
- *Country music.* In many areas of the United States, you might get very few requests for country music. In others, you might get nothing but a month of country-themed weddings. Showing that you can turn your DJ business from rock to country easily will make you marketable to many more customers. Country is a huge-selling market, and a lot of fans out there are looking for DJs for their reception. Show an understanding of current pop-country and country classics. You'll want upbeat, rock-country songs alongside slower, romantic ballads. You can tie these in to your line-dancing track as well.
- *An outro.* Make sure your demo has a sample "last call" and "thank you" to the crowd. Your potential clients will want you to help end the evening and let the guests know that the party is over—something the potential clients really don't want to do themselves. Sound professional and sincere and make sure to thank your clients, too, and congratulate them on their big event. This is your last chance to make a great impression at any event, and your demo should reflect your enthusiasm.

Internet Advertising

Think about the last time you spent a good chunk of time away from the Internet. For me, it's usually on long travel days when all I'm doing is seeing the inside of airports for hours on end. Other people are lucky enough to spend days at a time away from the Internet and the glare of computer screens. But for most people, the Internet consumes a great portion of everyday life, much more than is consumed by print media and other advertising mediums combined. The Internet is the new battlefield of business—and it's where businesses are made or broken. It's also never been cheaper—in many cases, it's free—to advertise on the Internet.

Being prepared to advertise on the Internet is absolutely nonnegotiable if you're starting a small business in today's economic climate. Let's take a look at the pathways you can use to leverage the Internet's free and next-to-free advertising mediums for your DJ business.

Basic Social Networking

In today's Internetcentric society, you'd be foolish not to take advantage of every social networking opportunity you have. It's never been easier to connect with people, market your product, and make a name for yourself—all without paying a dime. The social networking revolution has made it a lot easier for your clients to connect with you, share good news and positive reviews, and, most importantly, make informed decisions. You must make sure that your business puts its best foot forward in your social networking presence and builds upon both negative and positive customer feedback.

Don't Be "That Business"

How much social networking outreach is too much? When you're advertising via social networking, you've got to walk a fine line to avoid becoming a pest. Always keep the end user in mind—you're a consumer, just as your customers are. Think about how and how frequently you'd like to be contacted by businesses—and apply that same level of discretion when contacting your customers.

Building an online presence can be an intimidating process, but it's actually easy—just time-consuming. It's equally hard to come up with hard-and-fast rules for social networking; finding the right combination of activities to market your business in the social networking world is chasing a constantly moving target. That being said, it's not hard to get a good, solid start.

First, prioritize where you think your business should have a presence. A lot of social networking sites are out there, and many of them aren't worth having a business presence on—there just isn't the user base to make maintaining a social networking profile worth the effort, considering how often each site's presence must be updated to keep your information current. According to Internet statistics wizard Alexa (www .alexa.com), as of this writing, Facebook is the number one social networking site in the world, with Twitter and Myspace number two and three, respectively. Facebook is the primary social networking tool that many people—and businesses—use, so let's talk about building your business's reputation on Facebook first.

Facebook and You

Building a business page on Facebook is relatively easy. You need to provide well-written information about your business, what you do, with whom you've worked, and what exactly you offer. Making sure your copy is well-written is important—a business without well-written content on its web presence isn't taken seriously by most readers. Sharing photos on Facebook is also a great way to show off what your business does best, but make sure that your clients agree to have photos of their event shared online. Not everyone will.

After you've established your presence on Facebook, you can start adding fans—but be careful about spamming. As you probably know all too well, being spammed by businesses that you're not interested in is annoying. You don't want to be one of "those" people, do you?

Facebook can be a powerful tool for your business. You'll be able to talk directly to your customers, get their immediate feedback, offer specials and promotions, and—most importantly—find ways to serve them better. You'll have a direct link to finding out what they're liking and what they're listening to and—by having this knowledge—be able to stay ahead of the latest trends. Being able to come as close as possible to reading your clients' minds is extremely important.

Forums and Blogs

I remember the first Internet forums I was involved in, way, way back in the day, Prodigy had some amazing DOS-based bulletin board systems, and I loved perusing the message boards. Later, dial-up bulletin boards were all the rage. Today, those relatively primitive mediums of digital communication have given way to forums and blogs. Both forums and blogs are, increasingly, a smaller portion of the Internet's social media networks; most of the businesses who find success with Internet advertising have both a strong website presence and a presence on social networking sites. Still, forums and blogs make excellent platforms for both your business and yourself as a DJ.

Many of the top DJ forums on the Internet feature great conversation among DJs like yourself. You'll be able to network, show off your gear, and get advice from other pros in the field doing exactly what you're doing. You'll also be able to network with other DJ businesses in your area, and although they're definitely the competition, you never know when a friendly fellow DJ will call with a gig he or she can't make that turns into a reasonable payday for you.

Looking for some forums? Here's a selection of top Internet message boards for DJs, as of the time of this writing, most of which have been helpful resources in writing this book:

- DJ Forums: www.djforums.com
- VirtualDJ Community: www.virtualdj.com/forums
- Our DJ Talk: www.ourdjtalk.com
- My DJ Space: www.mydjspace.net
- Pro DJ Forums: www.prodjforums.com

Blogs are a different beast altogether. Most blogs shy away from advertising related posts, so your best use of blogs is to bolster your resume. Many blogs discuss the newest equipment and production techniques, and reaching out as a guest author on such blogs is a great way to utilize the blog format to gain exposure. Running your own blog on your website—as long as it's done in a way that appears genuine—is also a great way to connect with your clients. Establishing yourself as an expert with a firm, affirmative voice on your subject is a key marketing tool for any performance professional.

Craigslist

Some of the best clients I've had in my business have come from connections I've made via craigslist. Craigslist is an online classifieds website where businesses and individuals advertise a multitude of items and services. Craigslist.org is a popular web resource mainly because it's a free, easy to use, easy to read, and doesn't accept paid advertising for better posturing of ads. Craigslist is a great site because it's generally self-policing: Scammers and spammers are quickly dealt with on a community level, which keeps the ads high quality.

Finding a local craigslist site is easy if you're in a major metro area but not as easy in rural communities. You'll be limited to the craigslist site for the nearest major market, but that's also a great way to network with potential clients in your surrounding areas. Craigslist ads allow you to post photos and web links as well as to anonymize your reply-to e-mail address.

Some of the best free advertising that small businesses find is on craigslist, and there's a reason why many businesses refer to it by name. Find your local craigslist site by going to www.craigslist.org and searching for the closest list near you on the right-hand corner.

Promoting via Groupon

One of the biggest crazes in Internet marketing is the group-deal sharing site called Groupon (www.groupon.com). Groupon is a fun concept—every day, they offer location-specific coupons, which are mainly small businesses offering discounts on their products and services. While it may seem weird to offer DJ services for a discount via one of these sites, they commonly offer deals on coupons for expensive services or experiences—recently, I even saw skydiving offered on my local Groupon!

Groupon, and similar sites, works by offering a gift certificate with a certain value—say, $50—for a discount price, routinely 50-60% off of retail. That $50 gift certificate might end up only costing the customer $25, but they get $50 worth of services. Depending on how the deal is structured, you end up with 40 to 50 percent of the final purchase price. While it might not sound financially safe to offer $50 worth of your services for only around $12, there are ways you can leverage these types of group sharing sites to benefit your business. Most of these coupon buyers are new customers, and you can use this as an opportunity to provide a discounted service where you will likely get repeat business—if not from the buyers themselves, then possibly from someone at their event who hears your work. You can also use the coupons as a chance to upsell services—and some Groupons even come with the stipulation that the customer buy some services at the normal rate to get additional time at the discounted price. Your pricing structure is up to you; you might offer two hours of DJ service for $100—normally a $400 value!—with the purchase of two hours at regular price. You can structure the deal any way you want.

Many small business owners have found Groupon and similar sites to be a great way to get new and repeat customers. Remember, getting your foot in the door with customers, their guests, and the entertainment venues they host their events at is very important—and these types of discounts offer a way to guarantee that opportunity.

Twitter and Beyond

Twitter is another site that many businesses find useful. Via Twitter, you're able to share short messages—to the public, directly to other people, or in many other combinations—and it's a great tool for you to use to communicate with potential clients. Responding to inquiries quickly and accurately on Twitter gives a business a lot of legitimacy and gives customers a sense of security that their purchase of your services is worthwhile. Setting up on Twitter is easy—and adding other people to follow you is similarly easy. It's not necessary to be heavily active—just when you need to be or want to share something with potential clients. But having a presence, especially considering Twitter's number two spot in social networking, is important.

With all this talk about social networking, what about Myspace? Well, that's up to you. Myspace, as of this writing, is rapidly losing users, and its demographics are shifting toward younger users. It's rapidly losing a following of people looking for businesses and bands—they're more and more turning to Facebook and Twitter for these kinds of updates. It's up to you to decide if you'll connect with enough potential clients to make the Myspace time investment worthwhile.

Reputation Management

One fact that any business needs to understand is that, unfortunately, bad reviews do happen. Maybe you accidentally played the uncensored version of a song at a kid's birthday party; maybe you got a little too comfortable and drank way too much at that wedding gig the other night—both nightmare situations for a professional DJ to be in. A bad review is absolutely inevitable—and you'll have to deal with it the best you can.

Think about how you've been handled as a consumer whenever you've had a complaint about a business. Did the business respond to your complaint or leave you wishing you had never hired it in the first place? When you're facing negative reviews from customers, you've got to strategize to please them—or at least defuse the situation. First, identify how you can respond. Many websites, such as Yelp (www.yelp.com) and TripAdvisor (www.tripadvisor.com), allow a business owner to create a free account and publicly respond to a customer's complaint. This allows you to make a public gesture of apology and offer to explain and work out your issues with the public domain as your watchdog to make sure you follow through. It's never a bad idea to respond to a customer in public, if possible—doing so certainly shows that you're listening.

One of the first lessons in reputation management for any business to learn is this: **If you get a legitimately negative review, don't try to get the comment deleted—focus your effort on repairing the business relationship.** A site that deletes comments and reviews under pressure from businesses simply doesn't offer the consumer a good experience. Think about it: Would you take seriously a positive review if negative reviews weren't allowed to stick? That's not reading a review; that's reading advertising copy.

So, how can you best handle online complaints and bad reviews? Here are a few tips to keep in mind the first time a former client hangs you out to dry online:

- *Always try to reach out to the customer.* Your customers—past, present, and future—won't know that you plan to do better if you don't work hard to discuss the issue with them. The moment a bad review pops up, take the time to find a way to respond to the customer, whether in private or public. Make sure your customer knows you care and want to address the issue.
- *Honesty is always the best policy.* Did you screw up? Then own up to it. If the customer's complaint resulted from a miscommunication, and you think it's easily worked out, then by all means pursue a solution. Sometimes honesty and a sincere apology are all it takes.
- *Be empathetic, not defensive.* Being defensive can make potential future customers think you're trying to hide a corporate culture of mediocre work. Be empathetic to your reviewer's plight and try to find a common ground. If the reviewer sees you as an honest business, he'll likely understand the human element that sometimes makes things unpredictable. That being

said, ruining somebody's wedding reception won't be an easy thing to recover from—it's best to be humble from the beginning and to seek to address the problem. You can't always repair the relationship, but you can always try to repair your reputation.

06

Money Talk—
Financing and Contracts

By now, you should have the planning stages of your DJ business under way. You've written a business plan, you've started to see how the framework of your business is coming together, and you've started honing your marketing strategy as a DJ. At this point, you should be getting ready to actually open the doors. But before you do that, you'll need equipment. And equipment is expensive. Here's where we're going to talk about how you can find the money you need to open your business and equip it properly. You can fund your business in many ways—and even though today's economy has made it difficult for small businesses to obtain loans and credit, it's not impossible if you do everything carefully leading up to your application.

You also need to clear up a few small legal issues surrounding your business. Insurance—especially liability insurance—is extremely important for a business such as yours. You're going to be attending public events, interacting with the public, and using your equipment in other people's places of business. You need to have an absolutely ironclad insurance policy for your business because bad things can—and do—happen.

After that, we'll talk about contracts, which are something that you might not think are necessary, but as any small business owner will tell you, they can make things a lot easier when something goes wrong. Sure, you want to be able to trust that your clients will always do the right thing, but the reality is that you'll likely need to call upon the powers of a contract to remind a client of the boundaries and limitations.

This chapter gets into some complicated legal issues, and some of what we talk about will be in generalities. That's because I'm not a lawyer, and every city and municipality has different laws, regulations, and procedures. Before starting your business, you should always consult with a lawyer in your local area who is familiar with the legal process of owning and operating a small business such as yours.

Financing Your Business

Getting loans to do anything with is rather tough in today's economy. Although the situation has improved since hitting a low point in the late 2000s, it's still difficult for many small, upstart businesses to get the financing they need. A lot of the problem has to do with the high failure rates of small businesses: According to the Small Business Administration, in 2008, 627,200 businesses opened, while 595,600 closed.

Financing your small business is likely to be a challenge. The kind of financing you seek is going to depend strongly on your personal credit, the money you have in the bank, and the overall outlook for your business.

How's Your Credit?

Do you know where your credit stands? As an aspiring small business owner, you should make sure your credit report is as clean as possible. Contrary to what the Internet might tell you, you can easily obtain a free credit report once a year without incurring any obligation or handing over any payment information. Visit www .annualcreditreport.com and request yours for free. Remember that you get only one a year per each of the three bureaus unless you're denied credit. In that case, you can easily request a complimentary report on a case-by-case basis.

Note: www.annualcreditreport.com is the only site set up in cooperation with the government to offer free credit reports; most, if not all, other "free credit report" sites will require a credit card and a potentially expensive "free trial" offer.

You have a few options for financing a business when you don't have the cash in hand. First, consider a traditional bank loan. Although it is a lot harder to get—and even harder to get with poor credit—a bank loan based on your good credit alone will result in the lowest interest rate and the best possible terms of repayment. Traditional bank loans can be frustrating if you have bad credit. You'll likely get a high interest rate—a good-credit loan could be well less than 10 percent interest, and having bad credit will push you into the 20 percent range—and you'll also need a cosigner. Be wary of this. Having a cosigner is generally an easy way to make sure your loan gets approved, but having a cosigner can also create major repercussions between you and your cosigner (who usually is a relative) if things get rough and you miss payments. If you're sure you can make the payments, a cosigner will be your one and only key to getting your loan—but be careful.

If your credit isn't sterling, you might need to consider putting up some collateral of your own to fund your business's loans. Commonly, a collateral loan will work if you have a home, car, or other legitimately useful piece of property that's paid for in full. You'll use your equity in this property to back up the loan, which you still have to repay, with interest. This alternative isn't a great idea if you don't think your business has a viable chance of paying back your loans for one big reason: Whatever collateral you put up can be repossessed by the bank if you fail to make your payments.

You can use home-equity lines of credit if you own outright equity in your home. From the first day you own your property, anything you pay becomes equity. You'll be able to borrow the difference between what your house is worth and what you currently owe, either as a lump-sum loan or a line of credit, which you can use as you need it. Home-equity loans can be a good deal if you're able to repay your loan quickly or need emergency funds, but using them to start a business outright can be a scary proposition. The downside to this easily obtainable credit is the fact that if you default, you'll lose your home. And it actually does happen—I know someone who lost his home as a result of a failed business.

Avoid the Credit Card Trap

Although it's tempting, resist funding your business with credit cards. If you qualify for cards with zero-interest financing and can confidently pay back your bills quickly, then by all means, a credit card might be the best way to bridge some small funding gaps. But relying on a credit card to carry your whole business is extremely risky and, in today's economy, hard to sustain over a period of time. Your interest rates will be a lot less favorable than those of a bank or personal loan, and you can quickly ruin your credit if things go bad.

Insurance

Insurance is something that most business owners don't like talking about. Insurance is expensive, but although it's hoped that you never need it, the first time you do, you'll be glad you have it. And if you don't have it and still need it, you're going to likely lose your business and every penny you have fighting out your fate in the civil courts. Scared yet? Insurance helps minimize the impact of the worst when it happens—and as a DJ who specializes in coming to people's personal events, you need to watch out for a lot of things. Let's say your equipment is damaged by a drunken party guest—and you need to get that turntable replaced by next week's gig. What if one of your speakers falls down and hurts one of the guests, and you've got medical bills to pay? The what-ifs are numerous. All of these are expensive propositions if you're not covered.

Liability insurance is a tricky matter. You need to check with your local regulatory authorities to find out how much insurance your business needs to carry. Depending on your location, you could have to carry $10,000 to $100,000 of coverage, sometimes more. This coverage should be absolutely comprehensive and cover all types of situations. And make sure that any exclusions are detailed in full by your insurance agent.

Insurance: One Size Doesn't Fit All

Although most municipalities require liability insurance of some kind, the New York City metro area requires insurance coverage of $1,000,000. That is the highest in the nation—and every mobile DJ must carry that insurance, no matter what. Your local area, even if it requires less, may mandate that you carry that insurance, too.

Aside from insurance for your liabilities, the biggest element you need to worry about is your equipment. As a performing DJ who relies on complicated audio equipment day in and day out, keeping your equipment in good shape is of the utmost importance. But transportation and heavy use of this sensitive equipment—not to mention the occasional beer spill—can take a massive toll on both your productivity and your pocketbook. Insuring your gear against theft, damage, and failure is extremely important.

In buying equipment insurance, keep in mind a few things:

- Gear insurance needs to be comprehensive and to have deductibles low enough that you can replace your gear immediately. Avoid policies with deductibles that largely exclude small but essential items.
- Make sure you can add *endorsements,* or additional items, to your policy. You may need to add equipment for larger gigs, and you should be able to make a temporary increase (at additional cost) to cover this gear.
- Rental equipment needs to be covered, too. Make sure your policy covers rental gear, which you might need for larger shows.
- Request guaranteed turnarounds. Some equipment insurance companies have waiting periods, which can be devastating for small businesses that rely on equipment. Others will allow quick payouts with proof of loss.

DJ Associations and You

Many DJ insurance companies are run by or supported by DJ associations such as the American Disc Jockey Association (ADJA). These require membership in order to be insured and offer competitive rates compared with those of most commercial insurers. The other advantage is a support network of other professional DJs—something that can be well worth its cost in networking advantages alone. It's up to you whether you join an association.

Being a Business

Being a business is a lot more difficult than just finding what you're good at, opening the doors, and offering your services to the public. Starting your business and opening its doors to the public require paying some fees that you'll need to factor in when you're starting your business. Unfortunately, cities and states differ in their requirements for establishing a business. It could cost you next to nothing, or it could cost you several thousand dollars. The differences are too numerous to mention here, so check with your state's regulatory authority about what you need to do to meet your state's rules. But before you do that, let's talk a little more in detail about what it means to establish your business in the variety of different ways you can.

Sole Proprietor

Starting a business as a sole proprietor is certainly the easiest way. You don't need an EIN (unless you wish to establish business credit), and all you need to do is file a fictitious name registration with your state's regulatory authority. A fictitious name registration is quite simple and generally costs less than $10 to file. This is where you tell the government what your business name is (your dba or "doing business as") and how it ties in to you. Check out the Small Business Administration website at www.sba.gov/content/register-your-fictitious-or-doing-business-dba-name/ for more information on registering your name.

Being a sole proprietor is easy and simple when it comes to financial management (you file your taxes as usual and include your self-employment taxes; you report your business income as additional personal income). But being a sole proprietor is not without risk. In fact, watch out: There's nothing protecting you and your personal finances from collectors and judgments if things go wrong. That's why incorporating your business is the next step as your business grows. You'll also find that, as a sole proprietor, you'll pay higher insurance rates and have a more difficult time obtaining and keeping business credit on the merit of your business alone.

Corporation

Incorporating is the next step in becoming an established business, and it's a complicated process that generally requires the help of a lawyer or tax professional. Whether you choose to establish a traditional corporation or the easier limited liability corporation (LLC), it entails a lot of paperwork and tax complexities that vary by location.

Being a corporation gives you certain legal protections that any business could find useful. Incorporating means that your business will exist as its own entity and will be completely separate in both name and finances from you. That means that you've got an added layer of protection—by no means bulletproof but still protection—from lawsuits and liabilities.

Being a limited liability corporation is a little easier and less expensive, but the protections offered are not as comprehensive, and the tax benefits aren't as beneficial. Still, the protection and status earned from becoming an LLC far outweigh those of remaining a sole proprietor. You're still the owner, you still operate your business as an entity separate from yourself, and you have most of the protections from lawsuits and collectors that you get as a full corporation. Depending on your local laws, your LLC can be taxed either as a pass-through entity—meaning it's the same as being a sole proprietorship—or as its own corporation, which requires you file complete, thorough business taxes. The decision to fully incorporate or become an LLC is generally determined by what's best for the business's tax structure.

Do You Need a Lawyer?

One of the first things I did when starting my business was find a lawyer. It wasn't because I was being smart—it's because I got ripped off on eBay. That's right: I paid over $1,500 to someone who cashed my money order (stupid move on my part) and sent the money to an overseas account—never to be seen again. I had to demand repayment or the item I purchased, and a lawyer was the person to do that for me. I remember being exhausted by the process of finding and retaining that attorney,

---

Finding a Lawyer

So, what should you look for in a lawyer? Here's a quick checklist for finding the perfect lawyer for your DJ business.

❏ Does this lawyer have experience in small business matters?

❏ How many years has this attorney been practicing? Is he in good standing with the bar association in your state?

❏ Has this lawyer had any disciplinary issues with the court?

❏ Does the lawyer understand the entertainment business and intellectual property matters?

❏ Can you afford this attorney's retainer?

---

and by the time I was done with it, I had spent a lot of money to find out I couldn't get my money back anyway.

Having on retainer a good attorney whom you trust is invaluable. After you find someone you like, you'll be asked to make a down payment on her services, called a retainer. Whenever you call and request help or advice, the charge for the professional time it takes to help you is deducted from this credit. Most lawyers ask for a retainer in the $250–$1,000 range.

Other than representing you in court, a lawyer can be good for going after deadbeat clients and enforcing contracts with clients. Sometimes you'll be hired for a private event and run into problems with event space labor or unions—and a lawyer can take care of these issues easily and cheaply. Having someone on your side immediately is of great importance in today's sue-happy culture.

Contracts

The most important piece of paper you can have in your business is a contract. It could also be the most worthless piece of paper between you and a client, depending on the client's intentions. Even with contracts in place, disappointments and lawsuits happen, even if they're frivolous and without any merit whatsoever.

Your lawyer should help you draw up a contract. That's because, again, each city and state is different. You might request something in your contract that isn't enforceable by state law. Then you're in trouble because your contract wasn't anywhere near ironclad. Like I said before, contracts can sometimes be worthless, but they'll mostly be your best friend. Clients will take you more seriously and default on you less often if you have good, professional, and easy-to-understand contracts. Holding your clients to their contracts is the job of your lawyer.

Included on pages 60–61 is a sample contract for your reference, courtesy of a DJ business in Chicago. Keep in mind that this contract covers legalities there; it might not cover you. Please consult a trusted legal professional before using a contract you write yourself.

St. Louis DJ Service, LLC
A Missouri Limited Liability Company

Contract for Services and Performance

1. Under the terms of this agreement, St. Louis DJ Service, LLC (herein referred to as "DJ") agrees to provide disc jockey services to the following client (herein referred to as "purchaser"):

Client's Name:	**John Smith**
	6651 Delmar Avenue
	Saint Louis, MO 63130
Phone:	314-555-0000
Email:	john.smith.stl@mail.com

2. The DJ agrees to perform the following services under the following conditions:

Wedding DJ Package: **One hour of wedding ceremony music; Five hours of wedding reception, including dinner and social dancing music and emcee services; All sound reinforcement and lighting equipment.**

Agreed Rate: $795

3. The performance details are agreed upon as follows:

Performance Date:	2/14/12
Performance Venue:	Lumen Private Event Space
	2201 Locust Street
	St. Louis, MO 63103
	314-555-5555

Performance Hours: Set-Up: 12:00 p.m.

                                            Wedding Ceremony: 3:30 p.m.

                                            Reception Start: 5:00 p.m.

                                            Event End: 10:00 p.m.

4. Deposits. A deposit of 50 percent of the total balance due, **$397.50,** will be due no later than the execution date of this contract. Any and all deposits due will be non-refundable.

5. Payment in full. Payment of the remaining 50 percent is due within five days of the event.

6. Force majeure. The DJ will not be held liable for any failure to execute the event as long as the event is canceled for reasons beyond the DJ's control; this will include power failures, accessibility issues with the venue, and "Acts of God."

7. Any scripting or event details must be given to the DJ with five days' advance notice.

8. Purchaser is responsible for any damage or liabilities stemming from event guests interaction with the DJ or DJ's equipment.

9. Purchaser agrees that any disagreement stemming from this contract will be heard first via arbitration; venue and moderator to be selected by mutual agreement.

10. All parties involved with Purchaser's event agree that the DJ may use their likeness in photographs or videotape that may be used for promotional use only.

AGREED TO: _____ Date: _____

DJ: _____

Your Rates

Pricing anything for a business is simple: You can price only for what your customers are willing to pay. I did some hands-on research, and after asking several successful, in-demand mobile DJ pros, I heard answers all over the board. That's because I

Sample Price Sheet

St. Louis DJ Service, LLC
Price Sheet, Current as of 11/2011

Event Type	Includes	Price
Wedding, Weekday	Five hours DJing, PA, lighting, emcee services, one rehearsal (one hour).	$795
Wedding, Weekend (Fri-Sun)	Same as above.	$1,100
Private Event	Five hours DJ, PA, limited emcee.	$500
Additional Hour DJing	DJ services added per hour to existing package.	$75
Non-profit DJ Gig	Four hours DJ, PA.	$375
New Year's Eve	Five hours DJing, PA, lighting, countdown Emcee.	$2,000

Additional services:

- Lighting (to no-lighting package): $150
- Additional Microphones: $20 per microphone
- DJ Mix Recording: $50
- PA Rental (no DJ services, just PA): $200/night, $45/hour, minimum two
- Extra Rehearsal or Set-up Time: $35/hour
- Additional PA: Priced per individual event spec
- Travel: Travel is included within 200 miles of St. Louis, MO; additional cost of 50 cents per mile over 200 miles.

heard answers ranging from $100 an hour plus production and transport to $1,000 per event, all-inclusive.

On average, DJ services have a set fee for a minimum amount of time, and the fee includes the production equipment, your time and services, and transportation within a certain radius of your home. Any additional hours are paid at a flat rate. Any extra services can be priced on demand, and you might want to offer discounts for slower days of the week, keeping your premium-priced nights Fridays and Saturdays.

Setting your rate is an essential part of your business, and your pricing structure needs to be both comprehensive and easy-to-understand for your clients. Pricing yourself out of a market is a possibility to keep in mind, too—if you set your prices too high, people may not even consider if they can afford you or not. They'll simply go with one of the cheaper options.

As a professional DJ business, you're probably not going to be the cheapest option for people looking for entertainment for their wedding or event. That's because, no matter how hard you try, there are always going to be people who are willing to do your job for you—even if they're not nearly as professional or experienced as you are. That's upsetting, but think about it. You can't compete with the "friends and family" discount, and a couple who can't afford a DJ but can afford to rent a sound system and be their own DJ from their iPods will always take that route rather than pay for a compromised, cheaper version of your normal services. Don't set your prices with these people in mind, mainly because you need to always aim for the middle—the people willing to pay a reasonable rate for your services under reasonable terms and conditions. That's not to say that the high-end market isn't there—and you should certainly aspire toward that direction if you can—but pricing yourself to meet only those clients' needs when you've got a large amount of more modestly priced business opportunities is an easy way to lose money rapidly.

So, what factors should you take into consideration before giving a quote to a potential client?

- *What will the DJ be doing?* Will you be just playing music and making light announcements, or will you be the star of the show, expected to entertain the crowd and emcee the night's events? That should factor into your price.
- *How much equipment will you need, and will you need to rent it?* If your rig isn't big enough for a particular space, you'll need to factor in the cost of renting this equipment. You can upcharge your rental fee to cover the

added expense of moving and handling rentals a modest amount if you wish.

- *What level of participation will the DJ have in the scripted events, and will this participation require rehearsal time?* Rehearsal time is time that you could spend doing other paid gigs. You need to be compensated for time you have to put into rehearsing for the events.
- *What is the cost of transportation?* As of this writing, a gallon of gas in Chicago is $4.25. Factor in the cost of transportation, the cost of gas, and the cost of tolls, parking, and other miscellaneous travel expenses before heading out to a gig. You can quickly eat up your profits in travel expenses.

Invoicing

Ask small business owners to name the word that strikes fear in their hearts, no matter how big or small their small businesses are. No, the word is not *taxes*. It's *invoices*. Invoicing is one of the most nerve-wracking chores of any business, and you'll probably find yourself at odds with clients due to long-overdue invoices. Invoicing is billing your clients for an event, mainly trying to secure the remainder of a deposit or the full payment for services already rendered. I advise most new small businesses against extending credit terms to new clients—after all, a lot of desperate businesses out there are trying to gain free services and equipment by opening new credit lines and immediately defaulting on them.

As a service business, you should always send out invoices on a regular schedule. If you expect all invoices to be paid promptly, giving your clients a window of around two weeks from the time of receipt of your invoice to the time when payment is due is necessary—you can't spring invoices on clients at the last minute and expect an immediate payment, as nice as that might be.

Invoicing is easy—you send a bill to your clients, and they (hopefully) pay. If your clients don't pay their invoices, you have the right to sue them for failure to pay for services rendered. As we talk about in the next section, you'll likely want to collect up-front deposits from your clients; doing this will keep clients from leaving you with an unpaid invoice at the end of the day, and it'll certainly keep you from working for free.

Looking for help in invoicing? Here's a sample invoice that you're welcome to use with your clients.

Mobile Party, LLC

Please remit payment promptly to:

Mobile Party, LLC
16501 Broadway, Suite A
New York, NY 10019
212-555-1000

Thank you for your business!

EVENT: Jackson Wedding - Chris & Jenny Jackson
INVOICE NUMBER: 20110411
TERMS: 30 Days

DESCRIPTION	QUANTITY	UNIT PRICE	COST	
DJ Services, Fixed Minimum	4	$ 175.00	$ 700.00	
DJ Services, Additional Time	2	$ 90.00	$ 180.00	
Medium PA, setup & tuning	1	$ 500.00	$ 500.00	
Mileage	24	$ 0.55	$ 13.20	
Lighting Rental	1	$ 175.00	$ 175.00	
Less Deposit			$(1,000.00)	
		Subtotal	$ 568.20	
		Tax 8.25%	$ 46.88	
		Total	**$ 615.08**	

Deposits

As a service business that relies on booking hours-long events to sustain yourself, you'll need to consider always collecting a nonrefundable deposit for your services. The reasoning behind deposits is that, if your client cancels the event within a window of time, you'll still be compensated for not being able to sell your services to someone else.

Although you can run your business's deposit policy however you wish, deposits tend to be anywhere from 50 percent or more and are always due up front when the contract is signed. Whether or not you choose to refund a deposit at all is up to you and the policies you set for your business. Most DJ businesses demand a nonrefundable deposit to secure a date, with refundable deposits at certain intervals to pay off the total due before the event. If the event is canceled with a certain amount of notice, all deposits usually become nonrefundable. Again, it's up to you—and you might want to avoid a more restrictive policy that your biggest local competitor may require—but addressing the issue of deposits is a great way to make sure your needs are met even when a client disappoints you.

07

Whenever I think of taxes as a small business owner, I get nervous. So do many others. Taxes are confusing, frustrating, and sometimes expensive, especially in an economy in which you can't spare much. I've told so many other business owners my personal story—of how I screwed up my taxes really badly the first couple of times I filed them and of how doing that has caused me issues ever since. You don't want those problems for your business. The IRS can, and will, make your life a living hell if it needs to.

Although I spent a lot of time cursing the IRS (for mistakes that were my fault), I eventually learned to respect its role in my business. The IRS is actually a lot easier to work with than it lets on, and it really does have amazing resources for small businesses to learn exactly how the tax process works. There's absolutely nothing wrong with admitting you need help and seeking out the information from the IRS. Likewise, if you have problems paying your taxes, contact the IRS before you let the problems get out of hand. The IRS can, and does, take people's businesses and homes for massive back taxes.

Taxes—and finances in general—are some of the least enjoyable topics of conversation, especially for such a fun business as yours. Hang in there—we'll get back to the fun stuff soon enough.

Don't Be a Hero

Before we get into trying to understand the gritty details of the IRS, I want to take a second to persuade you to do something that I wish I had done a long time ago: Give yourself permission to hire a tax professional when you need one. You're going to regret getting stuck with an audit or, worse, a tax evasion trial. These types of situations are usually the absolute kiss of death for any business, large or small.

We'll talk more about the specific situations when you'll need to consult a tax professional, but please heed my warning: Unless you're intimately familiar with the IRS's rules, as well as your state and local tax structures, don't go to bat for yourself in an audit, and don't try to go head-to-head with an IRS agent if you don't know what you're doing. Don't think you can weasel your way out of a complex situation, and don't try to be a hero and fix everything without the help of a pro. I know that, as a small business owner, you're always tempted to fix everything yourself—after all, you're probably doing all the work by yourself—but take my advice. Don't be a hero when it comes to your taxes. If you're in trouble, get help from someone who knows what she's doing and can to sort out your problems. Ultimately, the cost of a professional charging you won't be nearly as painful as the cost of the IRS coming after you.

Mistakes Are Costly

Did you know that the penalties for messing up your taxes can be very harsh? Although most mistakes will get you a slap on the wrist or a payment plan and some fines, some carry penalties that go up to $500,000 plus jail time. You don't want that for many reasons, mainly because the finances of lots of people never recover from the IRS fining them heavily.

Good Record Keeping

Most people aren't perfect record keepers. I know some friends who don't save any of their receipts or bank paperwork—and then there are the people with stacks of perfectly organized financial records sorted by date sitting in their storage units. I'm somewhere in the middle—and most business owners I know are also fairly vigilant about their record keeping.

Good record keeping is essential to the health of your business's finances. In today's extremely competitive business credit markets, you'll really need to have impeccable records to obtain credit. Lenders will want to see your financial information—how much money you're bringing in, where it's going, and how your overall business financial health is trending. It's also necessary to have excellent records when it comes to your taxes. If the IRS comes after you because it's not happy with something on your return, you're going to have to work hard to explain yourself. Having thorough records makes things a lot easier—the IRS tends to need to know a lot of information when things go wrong.

When thinking about the types of financial data you need to always save, we'll focus on three areas: your income, your liabilities, and your assets. Those are the three areas that lenders—and the IRS—care most about.

But first, let's talk about documenting your income. For every paying customer you have, you need to document how much you're paid as a business. This is done with *gross receipts* or *income statements,* and they're generally easy to keep straight because most banks will now let you do this type of organizational work directly on their website whenever you make a deposit. Aside from this, keeping copies of all of your client invoices and all of your clients' receipts for cash received is important. First, the IRS will want to make sure that the income you're reporting can actually be accounted for in legitimate manners. Second, lenders will want to see proof that you're actually bringing in money—especially whether or not you're actually bringing in money to pay the bills you'll incur if they lend you money. The IRS will consider a lot of forms of receipts for cash received; just about anything that shows the source of the money that comes into your business will work.

Proving Your Income

Although your bank records that match up to receipts provided by you to your clients are the most foolproof way to document your business's income, you can also find acceptable documentation in lots of surprising places. According to the IRS, you can use anything from a handwritten receipt, a credit card charge slip, a canceled check, and even an IRS 1099-MISC form.

Aside from the cash you bring in, you need to document your business's liabilities and expenses—the costs you're incurring in the name of the business and the fixed costs of the bills your business has to pay. Both the IRS and your lenders will want to know the shape of your business's finances, and the best way to show them that is to add up your liabilities and subtract them from your incoming cash flow.

This is how creditors determine if you're going to be able to make any additional loan or bill payments if they give you money—and they'd like to see a long-term picture that trends positively. Remember that credit lending is basically an "educated guess" situation—lenders have to see the hard evidence and make a reasonable guess about whether you're worth lending money to.

Your liabilities and expenses are just as easy as your income to document. First, you'll need to be able to note your outstanding, floating liabilities—such as equipment payments and any other standing bill that you're in the process of paying off. The reason why you'll need to document your liabilities and expenses is a little more complicated than your income: The IRS doesn't really care how much your business is in debt—but it does care how much of those debt-related expenses you deduct. Deductions for money spent on your business's needs aren't allowed if you don't have proof, and proving your expense record is the only way to make completely legal deductions. The rules here are fairly simple: Any receipt, invoice, or bank statement (even a copy of a credit card slip) can be used as proof that you spent something for your business. Keep one thing in mind, though: The IRS isn't above questioning things in great detail, so the better paperwork you have on hand, the easier this process could be if it becomes a problem in the future.

Last, the IRS also takes a keen interest in the assets your business has. You should be able to tell the IRS, with a reasonable degree of certainty, how much your equipment and other business-related purchases are worth. You'll need to be able to tell the IRS where you bought each item, how much you paid, and how that investment has worked out over time. The IRS is a big stickler on accuracy—and without accurate information you won't be able to take deductions for depreciation.

Keeping Documents Safe

Although it may seem like overkill, you should hang on to your financial records (of any type), your original business plan (along with any changes as you go along), as well as anything tax-related for the duration of your business's life. You should also save contracts and other business-related records for up to ten years; banking paperwork, although instantly accessible to most via online services, should be kept in hard copy (or at least digital copy ready for printing) for up to three years.

[Your Business Name]

Assets		Liabilities	
Cash (bank accounts)	_____	Accounts Payable	_____
Accounts Receivable	_____	Short-Term Notes	_____
Inventory (if applicable)	_____	Amount Due on Long-Term Notes	_____
Prepaid Expenses	_____	Interest Payable	_____
Short-Term Investments	_____	Taxes Payable	_____
		Payroll	_____
Total Current Assets	$_____	**Total Current Liabilities**	$_____
Long-Term Investments	_____		
Land	_____		
Buildings (cost)	_____		
Less Depreciation	_____		
Net Value	$_____	**Owner's Equity**	$_____
Equipment (cost)	_____	(assets minus liabilities)	
Less Depreciation	_____		
Net Value	$_____		
Furniture/Fixtures (cost)	_____		
Less Depreciation	_____		
Net Value	$_____	**Total Liabilities & Equity**	$_____
Vehicles (cost)	_____		
Less Depreciation	_____		
Net Value	$_____	Current Date_____	
Total Fixed Assets	$_____		
Other Assets	$_____		
Total Assets	$_____		

Deduction Basics

One of the most helpful (and often abused) tax breaks is the good, old-fashioned deduction. Taking deductions—whether for equipment, consumables, or travel expenses—is extremely common, and smart (and sometimes crafty) deductions can help a new small business when tax season rolls around. The main fact to remember about deductions is that honesty isn't just the best policy—it's an absolute requirement. When you claim a deduction that you're not legally entitled to, you're stealing money from the federal government. And like any business or person who has money stolen from them, the government doesn't care for that too much. Taking deductions you're not entitled to is the number one way to get the IRS to target you for an invasive and potentially expensive audit.

As a business, you've got a lot of options when it comes to deductions. Deductible expenses include:

- *The start-up costs of your business.* In the year your business goes live, you can deduct up to $5,000 per instance of start-up expenses, along with an additional $5,000 for what the IRS calls *organizational costs*—these costs include legal and licensing fees for starting your business.
- *Start-up equipment.* All of the equipment—from mixers to headphones to live sound reinforcement gear—can be written off. In the first year of your business, you can deduct the full amount of your business's equipment. Although the maximum amount constantly increases as years go by, it's currently at around $250,000. This deduction is done through something known as a *Section 179* deduction—and it's not something the IRS makes easy to find. You'll need IRS form 4562 to make this happen. Look for this form with instructions on www.irs.gov.
- *Equipment depreciation.* Equipment used in your business starts to lose value the minute you swipe your credit card at the store. You can write off the amount of depreciation your gear suffers over the years, but it's not nearly as good a deal as the Section 179 deduction mentioned above. Your tax professional should be able to tell you which method makes the most sense for you.
- *Utilities and services.* You can deduct everything you pay to other businesses for their services that your business needs—these include your utility bills, cell phones, and other fixed services you require.

I'm sure by now that you get the picture—you're able to deduct a lot, if you have the paperwork to prove it. Your tax professional might be able to catch a lot of things—and as I mentioned before, the complexities of IRS tax code aren't something you want to tackle without the help of a professional.

Taxes for the Self-Employed

Earlier we talked about the fact that being self-employed changes the game in a lot of ways. Before, in the employer-paid working world, you had people to take care of everything. Payroll, taxes, and benefits all happened seamlessly and without any work on your part; you just showed up, did a good job, and the right things fell into place. Not so much when you're self-employed! Being your own boss comes with a lot of benefits, but it also comes with a lot of work. Filing taxes as a self-employed person is one of those sometimes-frustrating chores that you will have to handle yourself. You'll likely be, at first, filing as a sole proprietor.

Self-employment tax is the government's way of making sure we self-employed people pay our Medicare and Social Security contributions like typical 9-to-5ers. The IRS wants to see you paying 12.4 percent of your earnings to Social Security, as well as 2.9 percent to Medicare. Only the first $106,800 of your income is taxed at this rate.

State Income Taxes

Don't forget your state income taxes! Just because you're self-employed and file as a sole proprietor does not mean you don't need to make sure your state is taken care of. Some municipalities also have their own income tax you have to worry about. State and local tax requirements vary—and there are hundreds of rules, way too many to list here. Consult a local tax professional to find out what you need to do.

One of the more frustrating requirements that we self-employed folks face is the estimated income tax. The rule is simple: If you've had a tax liability in the last tax cycle and will owe the IRS at least $1,000 over the year, you may be asked to pay estimated taxes. These are assessed quarterly and are based upon what you had going on the year before. You'll have to make the estimate yourself, using your numbers from the previous year. Estimated taxes can be expensive—overestimate, and you owe a lot more money than you can afford; underestimate, and you have to come up with money at the last minute when your return is due.

Your EIN

Our friends at the IRS require you to obtain an employer identification number (EIN) if you're going to be hiring anybody for your small business. You'll also need an EIN if you plan to incorporate or do any tax withholding for yourself or your employees. Need credit? An EIN is the business credit equivalent of a Social Security number. You'll find a lot of businesses willing to get you an EIN for a fee; this isn't necessary because the IRS makes it simple to do it yourself—for free.

See "Registering Your Business" in chapter 4.

Accounting Practices

Before we get back to some of the more exciting stuff that comes with your new DJ business, we've got to talk briefly about your methods of accounting. The IRS loves good records, as we talked about before. Having solid financial records is the gateway to good business credit, too. There are two main types of accounting for small businesses, and it's up to you to decide which you're more comfortable with: *cash* or *accrual*.

Cash Accounting

Cash accounting is likely to be the type of accounting you choose. It's just like most people's personal finances: Your business will balance its income with its liabilities, using live, real-time data, and you'll know at any given time how much cash you have on hand. This is the easy way to do it; you'll need to know how much money you've banked, how much income you're making, and the expenses you have in your business. You'll add them all up and balance it all out, and that's the money your business has to work with. Yes, it's easy, and it gives you a full financial picture, but it doesn't take into account unpaid invoices.

Accrual Accounting

The less common (and more complicated) type of accounting is *accrual*. With the accrual type, you'll be doing a somewhat precarious balancing act with your finances. That's because accrual accounting requires you to be speculative about the access to funds you might have—and one of the biggest problems with using the accrual type is that it doesn't accurately reflect what's in your bank account, thus preventing you from making real-time use of your financial resources. Accrual accounting best works for larger businesses that routinely survive on extended (and extending) credit. That's because an unpaid invoice—although no good to you as a small business—still counts as income. With the cash type of accounting, you count invoices as they're paid and bills as they're sent out; with accrual accounting, a sent invoice is treated as if it's paid, and all outstanding invoices and liabilities are processed into the ledger in real time, whether or not the cash is there to justify the entry. Accrual accounting is not recommended for most small businesses because access to liquid cash is generally necessary—and at a premium. The electric company and your loan processor won't care if you've got a stack of unpaid (but not yet overdue) invoices; they care only if you can make your payments with cold, hard, spendable cash.

Regardless of which type of accounting you choose, make sure you keep good records and process all of your incoming and outgoing money carefully. You'll need to make sure you do everything by the book—and make sure you know how to account for all of your money, whether you're operating at a profit or a loss (as many small businesses do at first).

When to Ask for Help

Obviously, any chapter about money and finances must be written in a broad sense because every business situation is different. Many people enter a business—even one as fun and carefree as your DJ business—with the idea that they'll be able to run the business easily and without needing an expanded base of knowledge in one particular area. I'm sorry, but most small business owners realize that the hubris of thinking they know everything is one of the biggest mistakes they can make. If you mess up your accounting practices, especially when it comes to the IRS, you're in for a battle royal—whether it takes place between you and your overdue creditors or between you and the IRS in the tax courts.

Please take the advice of a small business owner who, like you, started out on this scary and often-misleading journey with a lot of hope and an unfortunate sense of knowing it all: **Do not be afraid to ask for help, and make sure you hire a professional at the first hint of a problem.** Do not allow yourself to fall victim to your own best intentions; it's your business, and you're responsible for its success or failure. Part of that responsibility is to put on the best show as a DJ that you can for both your clients and their guests. The other part of that responsibility is to know when to give up and ask a professional to step in. Doing so doesn't make you a failure—just a smart businessperson.

Should You Hire a Tax Pro?

Are you agonizing over whether or not to hire a tax professional? Here are a few questions to get you started. If you answer "no" to most of these questions, it's time to call in a professional to help sort out your books.

❏ Yes ❏ No   Do you understand your federal, state, and municipal tax codes— as they affect both you personally and your business?

❏ Yes ❏ No   Can you defend yourself in case of an audit?

❏ Yes ❏ No   Do you feel comfortable arguing tax law in front of a judge?

❏ Yes ❏ No   Can you explain every deduction you feel you're entitled to?

❏ Yes ❏ No   Do you understand how to deduct smartly, avoiding audit red flags?

Now that we've spent some time getting your business's more complicated (and, admittedly, tedious) aspects out of the way, it's time for the topics you've been waiting for. In the next few chapters, we'll be working on the specifics of actually being a top-notch DJ, starting with the equipment that you'll rely on to make your performances the best they can be. Then, we'll look into some of the finer points of being the absolute best DJ (and emcee) on the scene—and ways that you can leverage yourself as a top-quality competitor in your new business arena.

08 | Build Your Rig

Now that we've got a lot of the boring paperwork out of the way, it's time to start making sure you put your DJ rig together properly. This is where the fun stuff starts. This is what you got into this business to do, right? But before your first note hits your first event's dance floor crowd, you're going to need to make sure that your DJ rig is up to standard for all types of situations.

These days, simple set-ups of modest cost can still be extremely powerful, sound good, and travel reliably well. Technology has become a lot smaller and a lot more affordable. There's a lot of great gear out there to pick from, and it uses exciting digital technologies with price points at never-before-seen lows while offering quality that we've previously seen out of only high-level professional gear.

Let's look at the elements of an ideal DJ rig. And another note of warning: I'll mention some brand names, but things like these constantly change, so I'll avoid making recommendations only because I'd rather you keep two facts in mind:

- It's much more important to know exactly what you need, how the things you rely on work, and what their individual roles should be in your system.
- It's then up to you to take a snapshot of your budget and decide what you can do with your best interests in mind.

Another tip that I'd like to share with you is one that came from the many professional DJs I consulted for this book: Please avoid the "DJ in a box" systems that you see advertised for an unbelievably low price. These are generally low-level pieces of equipment sold at a premium to those who don't know better. It's much more cost efficient to piece together your own system for your specific needs, especially if you feel comfortable buying used gear. It's not a better deal to buy low-quality equipment; you're paying a lot for the convenience of someone putting it all in one box for you.

Your Format: Analog versus Digital

In the world of audio (and DJing in particular), there's not a single issue that starts more heated debates in audio "geekdom" than analog versus digital. Analog purists—those DJs who prefer spinning only vinyl—and those who embrace digital storage and playback technologies have long debated both the advantages and disadvantages of these methods of song playback. Analog purists say that their records offer a more unique perspective and a sound much truer to the master recording. Digital adopters state the most obvious fact: that when you're on digital, you can have limitless choices—something those DJs carrying those crates of vinyl don't have.

Whether you decide to be an analog or a digital DJ depends on your target market and demographics. Let's say you're planning to DJ just one genre in particular—be it blues, soul, jazz, or rock—and you'd prefer to play from only your library of vinyl. That's fine, but it's not a wise business model if you're planning on getting a steady business. Sticking to vinyl—as cool as it can be—limits your clients' choices severely. If your community is large and diverse enough for you to service a niche market such as this, then by all means pursue it, but keep in mind that this kind of decision should be made after careful market research.

Kickin' It Old School

A lot of people are making a fantastic living spinning specialty records on vinyl only. Soul, blues, and jazz records are the most popular. These types of set-ups are simple and generally consist of a pair of high-quality turntables and a simple mixer, along with cases of some of the best and most unique vinyl you can find in your genre. It's something to consider if your market can support it. If it can, and you can do it well, go for it!

All about Turntables

If you do plan to go the vinyl route, you'll need to start by getting quality turntables. Turntables are a hotly debated item because everybody's got a favorite brand that he or she is fiercely loyal to. Turntables can be expensive—some finely calibrated audiophile-quality tables run multiple thousands of dollars. In fact, I remember getting an e-mail ad for a turntable that retailed for close to $10,000! Such expensive turntables aren't necessary for your functions—in fact, the right turntables for you might cost less than $100.

The first question to ask yourself is if you even need turntables. They're not necessary unless you're looking to perform with vinyl records, something that can be fun to have but can be a lot more hassle than they're worth. Records are heavy, break easily, and generally can degrade over time with heavy road use. Digital storage eliminates all of these issues but doesn't give you the "cool" factor of vinyl. This all being said, keeping vinyl as an option isn't hard—it takes just a good turntable or two, space, and a good mixer—in fact, with most DJ mixers, having multiple source options—including vinyl—is as easy as flipping your crossfader.

If you've decided that vinyl is for you, here's what you should look for when buying a turntable:

- *Look for a sturdy, professional-quality turntable*. Brands such as Technics and Sony make some of the best turntables for DJ use; they don't run much money and will give you years of service with proper maintenance.
- *Seek out belt-driven turntables*. There are two types of turntables—direct-drive and belt-drive. Belt-driven tables make less noise and are generally more reliable. Most of your high-end turntables will be belt-driven.
- *Make sure your turntable has reliable outputs*. Some turntables have unreliable connectors; make sure yours has professional-type RCA outputs that will connect to your mixer. Also make sure your turntables have proper grounding connections.
- *Check your pitch control*. All good turntables will allow you to control the speed of playback, affecting the playback pitch. You'll need this feature to work with a variety of records.

Mixers

A good DJ mixer is an essential part of any DJ's live rig. A mixer takes all of your play-back sources—turntables, iPods, CD players—and allows you to select which sources you wish to play and how you want them blended and gives you the ability to cue multiple sources at once. Hundreds of DJ mixers are available for around $100 and up. Mixers can be simple or extremely complicated.

DJ mixers are a lot different than the standard audio mixers we use when mixing live bands. Those mixers have many channels—sometimes up to forty-eight microphone inputs along with some stereo returns—with multiband equalization on every channel. You'll also have various routing options, allowing you to make several mixes simultaneously, good for making monitor mixes for musicians on stage. DJ mixers are much simpler—they generally combine two to four stereo channels (either RCA or ¼-inch jacks), have a single microphone channel, and have functions to both cue and blend the different stereo tracks in headphones. These mixers are generally light and easily rack-mounted.

Getting the Most from Your Vinyl

If you plan to use vinyl, make sure your DJ mixer has RIAA EQ on the RCA input jacks. RIAA EQ is the standard way that a vinyl record's sonic signature is deciphered by the playback unit, and without it, your records won't sound right. Finding a mixer without it is rare, but just be aware of needing it in case you notice it's not mentioned on the mixer you're shopping for.

The feature that allows you to switch between sources is called the *crossfader*. The crossfader's health is important, and on the higher-end DJ mixers, this fader will be field-replaceable. Numark, Gemini, and Vestax are among the most popular choices. The crossfader, if dirty, can produce lots of noise (or, worse, complete loss of signal). Regularly cleaning and lubricating your crossfader will help keep it in good shape.

Aside from your crossfader, you'll have a fader representing each channel, be it a microphone channel or a stereo pair. These faders will be used to control the overall level of the selected channel in the mix that you're sending out. The idea is that you'll use the crossfader to blend between the two sources, and you'll use the channel faders to control the volume of each channel in the mix. Your faders will have the same importance as your crossfader, although their failure will also be an issue midshow.

Aside from the actual send you're feeding to your speakers, you'll be able to make your own mix, or a *monitor* mix. This will be fed to headphones or a cue *wedge*, or monitor speaker. You'll be able to send—known as *prefader send*—the signal of something you're cueing and blend it in your own headphones with what's currently being sent out. You'll be able to beat-match (and verify that the selected program is what you want) and then blend it into the overall mix.

From there, your DJ mixer should go into your audio system—more on this in chapter 9.

Storing Gear (and Being Roadworthy)

Your DJ gear is highly sensitive. And, now that it's your livelihood, you've got to realize that damaged gear means lost time and money. Making sure that your gear is ready to hit the road is one of the most important tasks that any DJ needs to pay attention to. Throwing your gear into the back seat of your car and hoping it arrives in one piece are the easiest way to find yourself without the gear you need (and without access to a replacement).

Making your gear roadworthy is generally done by properly mounting it in road cases. Most road cases are considered airline-safe, or *ATA rated*. *ATA rated* means that the Air Transport Association—a standards-setting organization for air-based cargo transportation—has approved a case to meet its standards for being used in heavy-stress air travel. ATA rating a case ensures it'll stand up to normal wear-and-tear on the road. Road cases purchased for gear that are not ATA rated will generally be flimsy—made of particle board or plywood—and offer little protection against the biggest threats to your equipment, namely shock from being dropped.

Road cases for your gear will not be cheap. The amount you'll need to spend on cases depends on your set-up—the more gear you elect to carry, the more you'll need to safely transport. Making sure that your gear is safe should be a number one priority.

Aside from transporting your gear, your cases should allow your equipment to be stored at your home without the outside elements becoming a problem. Whether you're storing in an on-site storage unit, your garage, or your climate-controlled home, your gear should always be stored in its cases to keep out dirt and dust.

Flying to a Gig with Your Gear?

Flying is a lot different than just tossing your cases into the back of your car. Airlines take little responsibility when it comes to checked baggage—there are limits for every kind of damage, depending on the airline policies at the moment. Having your gear properly cased in ATA-rated cases is the only way to ensure that if something does happen, you'll be covered—ATA cases can withstand a lot, and you'll rarely find yourself disappointed with the results. Take note that non-ATA cases won't qualify for some baggage insurance payouts in case of damage.

Digital Song Storage

Storing music digitally is, quite possibly, the easiest and most cost-effective way to carry a large music library with you at all times. As an event DJ, you must offer a large variety of songs on demand. Digital storage makes it easy to access everything in a matter of seconds.

Just How Many Songs Can You Carry?

How many songs do you think can fit on a regular hard drive? In today's world of high-capacity drives—one terabyte and greater—you can fit a lot of music. Figure on about 250 songs per gigabyte of space.

DJs can use a lot of software programs, like DJ Jukebox, to organize their music collection, and it's up to you and what you're comfortable with when it comes to what you use. These programs range in functionality from just simple organization and playback—just like iTunes—to extensive beat-matching and mixing applications as well. These software programs, likewise, can be free or cost quite a bit of money.

Your digital media should be stored on portable hard drives with some important factors in mind. The first is reliability: Making sure that your digital storage is reliable is important. Hard drives come in all shapes, sizes, and costs; the cheapest are not always reliable. Some of them aren't reliable at all and are prone to failure. Most of the name-brand hard drive companies—Seagate, Western Digital, Crucial, and others—offer much better reliability rates when compared with the generic competition. Spending a little extra money isn't such a bad thing when it comes to reliability.

When buying external hard drive storage, you need to keep a few factors in mind:

- *Always buy more than you need.* Digital storage is cheap these days, and the difference between 500 gigs and 1 terabyte can be really close—sometimes as little as $25. Make sure you buy for the future, not just for your immediate needs.
- *Buy a high-RPM drive.* Drives of 7,200 RPM allow you to access data a lot faster than the older, 5,400-RPM drives. Buying a higher-RPM drive will allow you to access songs faster on the fly—something that's important to you as a DJ.
- *Make sure your external hard drive is roadworthy.* Higher-quality drives will have more rugged enclosures that can absorb mild shock and keep things going if the unthinkable should happen to your storage during a show. Make sure you're not buying a flimsy enclosure.

Backups

Talking about data storage isn't complete without a quick note about storage backups. Whenever you buy hard drives for your DJ business, you should always make sure you're buying enough to have at least two backups: one backup that you store with you whenever you're on the job and the other a backup that you keep off-site, either in a safe location in your home or in a secure second location (one of my DJ clients stores his in a safe deposit box at his local bank). You should back up as often as you make changes to your library; all of your backups should be current at all times. Setting a weekly backup time is one of the best ways to do it—and you'll always know what day of the week your latest backup goes to.

Backing up is another way to keep things going if one of those worst-case scenarios happens to you. Data are easily lost, just as any piece of your hardware is. Making sure that you have access to a fresh backup quickly and seamlessly is absolutely essential. Don't get caught without your backups! Many DJs and audio engineers—myself included—have been stung by data failures.

Where to Buy

Buying DJ equipment is a major commitment on your part. Finding a good retailer with whom you can work closely to buy your gear is absolutely essential—in fact, I've always found it more logical to take the approach of *buy your seller, then buy your product.* **Always make sure you're comfortable with the level of presale and postsale customer service your seller offers you.** Asking for recommendations from other DJs and sound engineers in your area is an easy way to get set up with someone—either a direct sales rep or a point of contact—who can make your buying go smoothly.

When selecting your new DJ business's supplier, here are a few questions you might want to ask:

■ What kind of warranty do you offer on top of the manufacturer's warranty? Some sellers have the added benefit—many times at a slight disadvantage in price—of an additional warranty. This is something you might consider using for major purchases.
■ Do you offer any training or after-sales support?
■ What's your return policy? Make sure that you can send your gear back if it doesn't meet your expectations—and know up front how much doing this will cost you (most sellers will charge a restocking fee).
■ Can I trade in gear at a later date?

While we're on the subject of buying gear, please be careful if you buy gear via eBay. Although eBay is an excellent resource for used and refurbished gear, it can have a lot of traps if you're not careful. Always inspect a seller's feedback rating and make sure that the seller you're dealing with is legitimate and will allow you to verify that fact in some way before you send your money. If you're wary, always pay via PayPal and make sure everything is done through eBay's system. PayPal and eBay can't help you if they don't know every detail—and if you pay via a method other than PayPal, you'll be unable to get your money back if you do get ripped off. Be careful, and eBay can help when you need gear that you can't afford—but watch out at first.

Selling Gear

Gear generally has a limited lifespan, and when it's time to let it go—either because it's not working as well as it used to or you've simply outgrown it—selling it is generally the best way to handle disposition of your gear. Selling your used gear is also the quickest way to recoup some of your investment if you need a quick cash injection for upgrade purposes.

Remember when we talked about making sure your gear is roadworthy in storage cases? Your gear is a lot more valuable if it's in mint condition; even the normal road wear that comes from day-to-day use will be minimized if your equipment is stored properly. You will also need to make sure that your gear is well maintained—it'll keep its value much longer if parts aren't broken.

Selling your gear—especially if you choose to sell online—can be easy, and as an established business, you'll have your business's good name as your guarantee that you're selling something quality. Being a successful online gear seller means that you'll always be honest with your buyers and that you'll always make sure your buyers aren't taking advantage of you.

If you're going to sell some of your used gear online, especially via eBay, remember a few tips to make sure every transaction is successful:

- *Label and describe your gear accurately.* Make sure that you're listing the right model number and feature set for your gear. Make sure every function works as advertised and, if not, make note of it for the buyer.
- *Always accept cash in person.* If you're selling via craigslist or a local classified ad, you'll want to accept only cash (or credit cards through your business). Checks have a tendency to bounce.
- *Never accept a money order.* Money order scams are one of the most common traps to befall new sellers. You'll send the item and receive a bogus money order in payment—a money order that you won't know is bogus until weeks later when your bank account is turned upside-down because of it. Always accept trackable, refundable payment.
- *Ship promptly.* Always make sure you send purchases to their new homes as quickly as you can; doing this will help build your reputation as a quality gear seller.

09

Basic Live Sound Reinforcement

Live sound has come a long way in the last several years. Chances are that you've noticed this advance when you've been to a concert that sounded amazing or witnessed a DJ performance that had the whole room moving with a rock-solid sound system. Back in the 1970s, live sound started becoming both a science and an art—it wasn't about hacking together what worked anymore. Thanks to engineers like Bob Heil, the man responsible for some of the most industry-defining technical advancements in the history of the craft, we saw the development of equalization, clean mixers, and technology that we're still using verbatim to this day. Back then, and even until the late 1990s, live sound technology was heavy, relied on sometimes-unpredictable analog equipment, and required quite a bit of careful balancing to make everything work. Not so much these days.

Live sound today is much different than it was even ten years ago. Live sound systems are digitally controlled, lightweight, and pack a strong, reliable punch in small spaces.

Your sound equipment is a lot different in form and function than your DJing rig itself. This part of your system will control how your customers hear the work you're doing, amplifying the music and your performance as the emcee of the event. Some DJs prefer simple speaker systems, others rely on much more expensive and elaborate systems. With high-quality systems available for relatively modest budgets, there's no reason to carry inferior equipment with budget as your excuse.

This is a complicated chapter, but keep this in mind: Many DJs may not have the advantage of having an in-depth understanding of the live sound process and the physics and rules that go into it. Understanding these will give you a distinct advantage—because remember that it doesn't matter how many songs you have or how cool you think your emcee shtick is—if the sound sucks, your clients aren't going to be giving you a good recommendation to their friends (or, worse, will give you a bad one via the Internet).

Signal Flow Basics

Signal flow is the first factor you should understand as you begin your journey into live audio as part of your DJ business. Signal flow is the way in which the electrical impulses carrying your music and voice travel through your system, from the moment they leave your DJ rig to the time they hit your listeners' eardrums. Sure, it seems complicated, but sound is in our everyday lives—it's one of the big things that we take for granted. Learning how to better make and manipulate sound to be pleasing and safe to the listener is extremely important. Likewise, understanding how the electrical signal carrying audio travels, where it travels, and all the steps along the way is absolutely instrumental in troubleshooting any sound system.

Signal Flow of Your DJ System

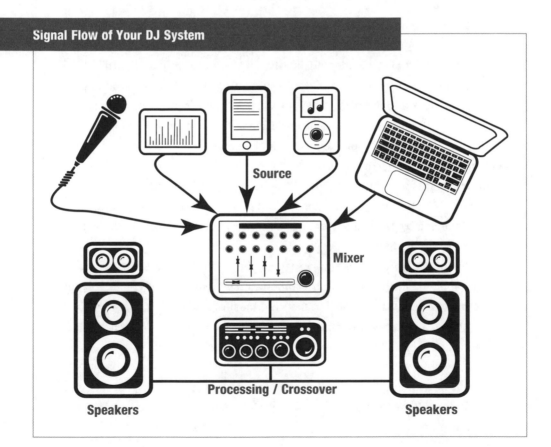

Source

Mixer

Processing / Crossover

Speakers   Speakers

Starting from the moment your sound leaves your DJ mixer, it has to travel through a rather complicated system to make it to your speakers and out to the listeners. From your mixer, your audio signal will travel to your signal processing—which is generally just a simple equalizer (a device that lets you fine-tune your audio system's response) or, if your budget allows, what we call a *DSP,* or *digital signal processor.* There are some inexpensive DSP units out there, and later we'll talk more in detail about what they, and EQ, can do for you.

When the signal reaches your processing, you prepare the signal to enter the speakers. The purpose of sending your signal through any type of processing is simple: Your signal must be able to be manipulated to take best advantage of the characteristics of the room and the speakers themselves. You'll have to do this processing because not every room is the same—and the way your speakers work depends solely upon how well you tune the signal to react with the room's natural acoustics.

After your sound leaves your signal-processing unit, it travels into your amplification system. An amplifier takes a low-level electrical signal coming from your equipment and makes it louder, driving the speakers with your audio. This stage in your audio equipment is important—without sufficient power, your signal will sound weak and distorted, and your speakers won't perform to their fullest potential. Different-sized rooms have different types of power requirements, which we'll talk about in more detail later in this chapter, and because of this fact, having flexibility when it comes to the scale of your rig is extremely important. Different spaces will always require a little tweaking on your end. Many speakers today offer built-in amplification, or you can go the traditional route of speaker cabinets driven by external power amplifiers. The choice is yours and defined by your needs and budget.

Your speakers are the last major part of your system. Speakers make everything happen, and they're the most important element when it comes to your customers' overall satisfaction. Speakers are the lifeblood of your operation, and they come in all shapes, sizes, and functionalities. They require a lot of heavy lifting and careful handling, but they'll be your most valuable assets when used day in and day out.

Signal flow is all about being efficient and making sure that your signal path is as clean as possible. Keeping all parts of your signal chain well organized is of utmost importance.

Good Signal Flow Checklist

Maintaining a good signal flow isn't hard, and it takes just a little organization. Here are a few tips to make sure you're taking the right steps when setting up your system.

❏ **Label everything.** It may sound like amateur-hour material, but labeling all of your cables—and making sure you know where each one leads—is the first step in building effective signal chains. Make sure you can identify, detach, replace, and repair any element immediately and with little downtime.

❏ **Keep spares.** One of the most important things to remember is that, at 10:00 p.m. on a Saturday night, there's nowhere you can run for a spare fuse, audio cable, speaker cable, or speaker. If one of your major elements goes down, you'll lose a huge part of your show and end up disappointing a client and end up costing yourself money in lost business if you can't get back onto your feet immediately.

❏ **Keep up on your maintenance.** Over time, your equipment will acquire the battle scars of hundreds of bar mitzvahs, weddings, and corporate holiday parties. Making sure that equipment is maintained, both internally and externally, will ensure that you won't have much to worry about and that you'll be more in control of what equipment is replaced and when. This helps prevent downtime and high costs of emergency replacement.

❏ **When troubleshooting, always start at the most likely source.** Each piece of your equipment should be able to tell you if it is receiving signal or not. Start at the top, and work your way down your carefully labeled and organized signal path. Find where you're losing signal, and troubleshoot the element. Don't waste time trying to craft grandiose solutions to otherwise simple problems; take your time, zero in on the suspect element, and swap out with a spare. You'll be in great shape.

Feeling the Beat

Whereas a modest system's signal chain is quite simple, many live sound systems used by DJs and live audio engineers are quite a bit more complex. For example, a top-quality Vegas-style dance club might have multiple digital signal processors feeding a wide variety of speakers sprinkled throughout the club, each delayed to match precisely so you don't hear weird phase issues when the signals overlap. There might even be subwoofers built into the dance floor so you're feeling the beat, literally, right through your feet. These installations sometimes cost in the millions of dollars and are extremely time-consuming to maintain. When you're troubleshooting your simple two-speaker system, keep in mind how easy it is in comparison!

Now let's talk about each of those elements in your signal chain and what you can use them for.

Speakers and the Basics of Sound

Aside from the music you play, speakers are the most important elements when you present your work to clients. Speakers are surprisingly simple but have extraordinary function. They're everywhere in our daily lives—from our cell phones that are tied to our ears around the clock to large concert systems. Speakers make possible every reproduced sound we hear.

Some speakers are higher quality than others; we refer to some speakers as *limited range*, which means they can produce only a narrow spectrum of audio. That spectrum generally depends upon their overall functionality—for example, a telephone speaker is a limited-range speaker in that it delivers only enough frequency response to present a listenable approximation of only one function that you're reproducing. These are the types of speakers you see in cell phones, toys, and other miniature devices that produce sound. These aren't the kind of speakers you need for your applications, but it's worth mentioning. The speakers that we use to reproduce acoustically accurate sounds are called *full-range* speakers, ones that, either through a combination of multiple *drivers* (the speaker elements themselves) or a single full-range driver, produce full-range audio.

When we talk about audio being full-range, we need to first understand how speakers work and how their results are measured. Speakers produce the vibrations that our ears in turn decipher into sound; those vibrations are different particles of air being moved at different velocities, and the size and speed of those vibrations are what we know as *frequencies*. We call them *frequencies* because you're measuring the *frequency* of vibrations within the sound waves; lower frequencies oscillate at less frequent intervals compared with higher frequencies.

Frequencies are measured by a unit called *hertz*, abbreviated as *Hz*. You're probably used to hearing this term applied to computer processors in terms of gigahertz, but when we talk about audio frequencies, the most we go up to is kilohertz, meaning thousands of cycles per second. We don't talk about gigahertz because of our physical limitations as human beings. Sound waves, regardless of how high we can make them go in laboratory testing, can be deciphered within only a narrow spectrum by our ears.

The normal range of human hearing—in a perfectly healthy ear—is around 20 hertz to 20 kilohertz—meaning a pretty wide spectrum of audio. By the time most of us are in our late twenties, we've lost most of our ability to hear accurately between around 16kHz and 20kHz; in fact, as we get older, our high-frequency hearing progressively becomes duller.

Understanding all of this is important when you select speakers. Speakers have a listed *frequency response,* which is how well they do at reproducing specific frequencies. Many cheaper speakers don't accurately reproduce the highest, crispest highs and the dance floor-moving lows that you might expect. Searching for speakers that have good frequency response characteristics—close to 20Hz to 20kHz—is important because they allow a flat, customizable response that will shine in any acoustic space with a little work on your part.

Your full-range speakers will generally be either single-driver, dual-driver, or triple-driver. *Dual-driver* means that you'll have a separate low- and mid-range driver, coupled with a tweeter speaker—a speaker designed to reproduce only the highest frequencies. Triple-driver speakers add a dedicated mid-range speaker to the mix. These different elements are fed by what's called a *crossover,* an electrical circuit or device that separates frequencies and directs them to only the speakers they're meant for.

When shopping for speakers, you should remember a few considerations:

- *Do you need powered or not?* Powered, or *active*, speakers contain a built-in electronic amplifier. You simply plug it in, turn it on, and you're off and running. These are the most popular types of speakers for DJs. If you're buying unpowered, or *passive* speakers, you'll need to also buy a power amplifier capable of pushing the speakers properly and cleanly. Powered speakers themselves are the best way to get everything in one package, but you do lose the modular flexibility of having a separate power amp. The choice is yours.
- *What size spaces do you need to cover?* Depending on the size of most of the rooms you work, you'll need to make sure your speakers are up to the task. Bringing a small set of speakers into a big room is a quick way to make yourself look like an amateur. Make sure the speakers you buy have enough coverage for the average-sized room you generally see. If you have a room too big for your rig, you may be able to easily rent the gear you need, so keep that in mind when purchasing, too.
- *How do the speakers sound?* Most importantly, never buy a speaker until you've heard it in action yourself. If you don't get a chance to hear the speaker you're buying before you get it home, you'll never know if it's what you want. Knowing what a good speaker sounds like is absolutely essential. Always audition your speakers before you agree to buy them.

Headphones

If you think about your typical performing DJs, they probably have headphones around their neck. There's a reason why DJs and headphones are inseparable: You'll need to use your headphones for cuing up songs and making transitions as seamlessly as possible. There's no other way to listen discreetly.

Good headphones are essential. When working on your budget for must-have accessories, you should budget between $100 and $200 for a good set of headphones. There are a lot of great brands of headphones—Sennheiser, Shure, and Sony make some of the top models used in DJ booths everywhere. Good headphones won't break easily—and the cheaper models typically have a short lifespan in the hands of a busy DJ.

When shopping for headphones, here are a few rules to consider:

- *Make sure your headphones are easily driven to loud volumes.* You'll need to hear clearly and accurately over the relatively loud volume of your speakers and the reverberations of the room.
- *Check the frequency response.* Although you can't know for sure without auditioning them yourself, your headphones should state a reasonably flat response rate; something like 20Hz to 20kHz is common, with some headphones stating a response dipping down as low as 10Hz.
- *Make sure the cable of your headphones is long enough.* Some headphones built for the consumer market assume a distance only to your back pocket (and thus your iPod); this length isn't useful when you are standing and moving around a busy DJ set-up. Make sure your cable is professional length—6 to 8 feet. Many DJs also look for headphones with field-replaceable cables to avoid being without headphones if they manage to damage or break the built-in cable.
- *Look for a good, isolated fit.* You'll need to seal out a lot of volume around you—and headphones with "closed ear" designs will help. Noise-canceling headphones aren't necessary and are a waste of money in this scenario; find something that offers good hardware-based isolation, and you'll be fine, no matter what volume you're mixing at.

In-Ear Monitors versus Headphones

In the last few years, several top DJs have transitioned to using custom-fit in-ear monitors, or IEMs, instead of headphones. Custom IEMs are small earphones which are custom-fit to the user's ear canal, and offer astounding isolation and acoustic control—as much as 26 decibels of reduction in ambient volume, depending on the material which the monitors are cast. In-ear monitors require an audiologist to make custom impressions of your ears, which are then sent to the manufacturer's lab for casting, a process that can take up to a month. The brand with the most recognition among performing artists, DJs, and audio engineers is Ultimate Ears (www.ultimateears.com); all of their custom models offer specific frequency tunings, allowing the performer a choice of sonic flavors in their monitor. Club DJs love the bass- and low-mid heavy UE-7 Pro ($799); most others find the neutral Ultimate Ears Capitol Studios Reference Monitor ($999) to be perfect for their tastes.

Hearing Conservation

Before we go on, I want to make a quick note about protecting the most valuable asset to your DJ business. No, it's not your mixer or your music collection, although those are essential, too—I'm talking about your ears. Without good hearing, you can't have a career as a DJ. It's just that simple. Another startling fact is this: Without hearing protection, your constant exposure to loud sounds can be potentially devastating. After your hearing is gone, even a little bit, there's nothing anybody can do to get it back for you.

When you're exposed to loud sounds continuously, you can develop hearing loss—either by the deadening of your high-frequency response or by a constant ringing in your ears, called *tinnitus*. The number one fact about conserving your hearing is this: Time plus exposure equals loss.

Those who have employed your services depend on you to watch out for their hearing safety, too, although their overall exposure is generally less than yours because they—unless they're having a busy wedding season—won't be exposed as frequently as you are.

The first thing to do is to monitor your exposure. Buy an inexpensive SPL (sound pressure level) meter. This meter can cost as little as $10 for a fully functioning iPhone app to over $100; Radio Shack makes some excellent units for under $50. Monitoring your SPL during an average performance is important; at 100 decibels and greater, you're safe for only around two hours. Lower the overall level to 95 decibels, and you double your exposure time to four hours. Ninety decibels—a reasonably loud performance for most small spaces—is fine for up to eight hours.

If you're going to perform in high-SPL environments, invest in some good earplugs. Custom-fit earplugs by companies such as Future Sonics, Sensaphonics, and Ultimate Ears—around $150 plus around $50 in fitting fees—are an excellent idea. These offer nine to twenty-five decibels of filtered protection, allowing you to hear the music just as you intended it.

Remember that sound exposure is the number one health risk of your new career as a DJ. Protect yourself—don't let your hearing, and your career, be cut short because you weren't paying attention.

Cabling

Cables are an often-debated part of any audio system. A lot of audiophiles and sound engineers think that expensive cables make a huge difference in the quality of audio. Many others think that cable quality doesn't differ much as long as the build quality is high. Surprisingly, even generic cables tend to sound good—it's build quality where the more expensive brands win.

Think of your cabling as your essential link between all of your components. Your speakers will have to connect to your amplifiers or processing gear; your mixer will have to connect to your amplifiers, and your microphone will have to connect to your mixer. Everything requires cabling. These different components require different types of cable, and your individual set-up will determine what you need to buy. Buying cables doesn't have to be expensive, no matter what your dealer tries to tell you.

When buying cables—whether for microphone, speaker, or power—keep these tips in mind. You'll save a lot of money and have a strong rig that'll stand up to road wear.

- *Brand name isn't always better.* Cables can vary quite a bit in internal construction, but few of those proprietary technologies that the brand names sell have anything to do with the basic operation of the cable. Making sure that the cable you're buying is well-constructed is way more important than knowing who made it.
- *Connectors should be high quality.* Good, clean connection with no looseness is the absolute goal of a good-quality cable. Connectors made by companies such as Whirlwind and Neutrik are considered some of the highest in connection reliability.
- *Consider making your own.* Knowing how to solder your own cables— learned from many Internet sites—is a cost-saving measure that can actually result in much higher-quality cables than if you'd bought them premade. It takes a steady hand, but having the skills to repair cables in the field when you're stuck without a backup can help save a gig—and a paycheck. And that leads us to . . .
- *Always buy backups.* Make sure that you carry several backup cables for every function you have—you don't want to be stuck without something you need. Like I've said before, Guitar Center isn't open at 10:00 p.m. on a Saturday night when you've got an important gig to DJ. Making sure you show up to every gig prepared and ready for any situation is important.

EQ and Room Acoustics

The topic of room acoustics is a complicated one. Working in as many rooms as you do as a DJ requires a great deal of knowledge about how to deal with—and make the best of—the acoustics in any given room. There's a lot about a room that you, as a guest DJ, can't change: The decorations were set by the party you're working for, the room's construction has been a done deal for ages, and there are no options for bringing acoustic treatment into a room on short notice and with no budget. Making the best with what you have is extremely important. We all have been to those events—rooms where the cavernous reverb ate up what little power the speakers were putting out or where the bass heaviness gave you a serious headache midway through the party.

Although we could go on and on about how to correct problems in a room's acoustics, it should always be assumed that when you show up to a gig, your equipment will be in fine working order—that's the first thing you can always do to prevent a bad-sounding night. Even with challenging acoustics, having your gear working properly will give the event a fighting chance, even if the acoustics are stacked against you.

EQ is your most important ally in the war against room acoustics. Being able to tune out frequencies that can be problematic—thumping bass, a nasally mid-range, or extra-reverberant highs—is absolutely essential.

Earlier we talked about how signal processing is part of your overall signal chain in the live sound reinforcement portion of your rig. After you have your signal leaving your DJ mixer and out to your speakers, you'll need to manipulate that audio to sound great in the room that you're working in. Equalization is one of the most essential technicalities for any audio engineer to grasp.

In the live sound sense, EQ is used to take the signal that you're sending through your speakers—the music and announcements—and make it work for the room through the speaker system you're using. Using EQ takes either a good ear or a hardware tool that's known as an *RTA*, or *real-time analyzer*. EQ should be used to correct any frequency issues presented in either the speaker hardware or the room itself—correcting the sound to be more "perfect" to the ear of the listener. You'll usually need to tweak problem areas to make rooms work—compensating for acoustic buildup of low, mid, or high frequencies.

EQ of the type you'll want to buy for your rig comes in two forms. First is a simple, analog EQ called a *graphic equalizer*; graphic EQ is represented by multiple frequencies—usually thirty-one bands per channel—which can be added or sub-tracted easily. Digital EQ comes in the form of digital signal processors. These can be simple digital EQs or more complex systems, such as the DBX DriveRack system. These more complicated (but still easily configurable) systems allow a great deal of flexibility, including the option to do one-touch instant EQ of a room.

Using EQ takes a gentle touch. First, listen for the problems you hear using tracks that you're familiar with—and using that good pair of headphones you bought for DJing is a great way to do this—and listen to how the tracks sound in the room with your EQ flat. Then, using either an RTA or your ears, find the frequency ranges that sound "out of place." Gently subtract those frequencies, and you'll begin sculpting the frequency response of the room.

EQ Know-How

After you've got something listenable, keep in mind a few rules about EQ:

- You may need to keep EQing throughout the night. Humidity, the number of people in the room, and many other environmental factors will affect how the sound will present itself to the end listener. Keep your system changing as the night goes on to deliver the best experience possible.

- Always rely on your ears. If you think something is off—even if an RTA tells you otherwise—take steps to fix it. Sometimes electronics don't paint an accurate picture of what you're hearing, especially if you are using a cheaper analyzer.

- Remember to match your gain. On most EQ systems, you'll have the option to add gain—"make-up" gain—to your output signal before going to your ampli-fiers. Subtracting frequencies via EQ will always bring the overall volume output down; bringing up the output gain on your EQ will make the corrections as trans-parent as possible.

- Don't rely on a preset EQ curve. It might be tempting—and a lot of DJs think they have the "magic curve" already drawn into their EQ—but every room demands a different curve. No two rooms are exactly alike, and a variety of things can make the EQ job you did in another room sound absolutely terrible in another. One size does not fit all.

Microphones

In addition to playing enough variety of music to make everybody happy, being a DJ includes the task of being the event's emcee—the guy or girl who runs the whole show, keeps the event paced, and makes announcements. As such, you'll frequently be asked to allow other people to make announcements, give speeches and toasts, and find new, drunken ways to abuse the availability of a microphone connected to speakers.

Microphones are an essential part of any DJ rig. Generally, DJs prefer wireless microphones—wireless mics allow people to communicate anywhere in the venue, and you can include more people around the room who wish to say something. A wireless mic also lets you—the star of the show—move around and interact with the crowd.

Finding a good wireless microphone is easy. Brands like Shure and Sennheiser offer high-quality wireless vocal microphones with good range, good sound quality, and stellar build quality for $250 to $300. You can go up from there—and multiple-transmitter systems are also popular for putting multiple microphones on the floor at once.

Wireless microphones are battery hogs; finding units with rechargeable battery capabilities will be the absolute best route for you, but be careful—some of these rechargeable batteries have a much shorter life between charges than do alkaline batteries. If you go with a wired microphone—something like the Shure SM58, Heil PR-22, or the Sennheiser E835—you'll be looking at a lot less money but losing a lot of portability. A long cable—50 feet being common—is also necessary to get those speeches and toasts away from your booth.

Ultimately, what you buy is up to your budget. Your DJ mixer will have an input for your microphone, and all you'll need to do is gently EQ your microphone channel to avoid feedback—the high-pitched ringing you hear when a microphone hears itself through a speaker.

When buying a microphone, consider the following selling points:

- *Always avoid omnidirectional microphones.* Any microphone used for live vocal performance—such as your emcee show—should be a cardioid or hypercardioid microphone. These microphones have the ability to reject feedback by the heart-shaped pickup pattern, making it a lot easier to control in a noisy environment. Omnidirectional microphones—although cheaply sold with most value-branded systems—are useless in a live setting under most conditions.

- *Determine if wireless is for you.* If it is, make sure you're buying something that's not out of your price range but still feature-packed. Cheap wireless microphones sound terrible, have high susceptibility to radio frequency disturbances, and don't last as long between battery changes. Wired microphones are easier and more reliable, not to mention less expensive; the cost difference is usually worth it for the professional appearance of wireless.

- *Always bring a backup.* Never leave home with only one microphone. It's an essential part of your show—and just as everything else in your rig, it could break down when you need it.

Radio Frequency

Now that we've talked about wireless microphones, a little note on radio frequency. Whenever you use a wireless product—be it a cordless phone at home, a wireless microphone, or anything else requiring space on the airwaves—you need to make sure that it's free from frequency interference in order to work properly. Frequency interference is increasingly an issue, given the large number of wireless devices—including networking, cellular phones, and television transmissions. The FCC hasn't made it much easier for hobbyists and audio professionals, either.

Whenever buying a wireless microphone, first of all, check the frequency against known channels in your area. Digital TV channels are one of the biggest sources of interference in the 600mHz spectrum. Any product you buy should be frequency *agile,* or able to switch frequencies against a bank of presets that can help avoid frequency problems.

Before you start any gig, you should check your wireless equipment for interference and make changes if necessary. You may find that one frequency works for you all the time—and that's great, but rare. Many times DJs traveling outside their home area have difficulty finding clear frequencies if their equipment is limited to one or two options.

How can you check if your wireless microphones are going to be a problem in your area? Shure—one of the world leaders in wireless microphone technology—has an excellent tool on its website to help you find the information you need. Find it at www.shure.com/americas/support/tools/wireless-frequency-finder/index.htm.

When to Rent

Renting gear isn't always the best option—or the cheapest—but sometimes it's absolutely necessary. Sometimes you'll need to rent equipment to make up for features your set-up lacks, mainly in the sound reinforcement department. A big room, a lot of people, or a unique acoustic situation can make it necessary to either replace your sound reinforcement rig completely with rental gear or rent additional equipment to make it work for the situation you've been handed. Larger sound systems can become necessary if you think your system can't reasonably throw enough power to reach everyone in the room.

Thinking about renting gear for your next gig? Before you present this option to your client, think about a few important points:

- *Will the equipment rental be financially feasible for your client?* If your event fee is only $3,000, but your equipment rental is going to run an additional $1,500, your client may decide to go with a cheaper solution—probably a competitor with a bigger system. Make sure that you add rental costs to any quote you give a client up front. Surprises lose clients.
- *Can you afford to replace the gear if you break it?* The gear you rent is as good as yours if you break it. You'll have to be covered somehow—whether it be with a credit card (usually rental houses will hold the full value of the gear as a deposit via credit card), cash, or insurance. Make sure you can afford to replace any gear you might ruin.
- *Does the gig really need it?* Carefully examine the capabilities of your gear. If you can milk some extra volume out of your system by making some (safe) changes to your configuration, then do that rather than suggest rental gear when it's not completely necessary. As a good DJ, you want your performance to sound its best—but don't push your luck at the expense of your clients.

Engineering Your Lighting Set-Up

Now that you've gotten your journey to sonic perfection started on your live sound rig, it's time to talk about another important part of your DJ rig: lighting. Lighting systems aren't always necessary, no matter what some DJs will tell you; it depends on your client, the venue of your event, and the budget you've been given. Lighting is one of those things that many DJ companies tend to do poorly. Lighting equipment is expensive, fragile, and tends to take up a lot of time to get working properly if you don't take the time to configure it before heading out into the field. There's also the upkeep and maintenance involved—although with LED lighting becoming popular, both transportation and maintenance of lighting has gotten easier.

Many clients will tell you ahead of time if they need lighting, and you should be prepared to offer it if they ask. Many venues will already have high-quality lighting, and you shouldn't interfere with that; your four par cans on a stick won't look very professional compared to the venue's pre-set system. But some events—school dances, private parties, some commercial venues—won't be providing lighting, and that's your moment to shine.

Some DJ companies choose to charge additional rent for their lighting system, while others bundle the price into their overall package. Of course, it's up to you what your business chooses to do; many also favor offering a small lighting system complimentary, while charging for more advanced systems. You might also want to make sure you're not stepping on any toes by bringing your lighting system into the venue: many larger event halls actually have union contracts, and they'll demand that the event use their lighting people.

Get to Know Your Lights

Now, let's take a look at the different types of lighting systems you'll be looking at when you assemble your first lighting rig.

- *Parabolic Stage Lights (or "par cans") and "Beamers."* In the last few years, stage lighting has started to transition from hot, heavy parabolic bulb-based lights (called "par cans") to more efficient, lighter and more temperature-friendly LED lights. LED par cans and panels offer astounding flexibility—multiple colors in one light, whereas old par cans generally required the constant changing of colored plastic sheets in order to change the lighting color. As digital lighting systems get more and more sophisticated (and, lucky for us, cheaper), old-school par cans disappear at an alarming rate. Par cans, or their LED counterparts, focus light onto one area of the stage; these generally come in red, green, and blue shades; they might also offer different colors alongside standard RGB, but those three colors are considered the "base colors" of a good lighting rig; mainly, a well-tuned par can system with red, green, blue, and yellow lighting can create a combination of just about any color of stage wash. Par cans and beamers are generally focusable and offer great flexibility. Pars, LED or bulb, cast a single color over a wide area, whereas beamers do just what it sounds like—they beam a light directly to a pre-set area.

- *Strobes.* Strobe lights are ever-popular on the dance floor. These are the bright white lights that flash brilliantly at timed intervals, generally giving the illusion of slow-motion. Strobes are fun when used in moderation, and they're something that your clients might request. LED strobe lights are becoming very popular, just as with par cans; however, you might want to test out your LED strobe function before committing space for it in your rig; many LED strobes don't put out nearly the candle power of an old-fashioned, bulb-based strobe. Strobes, like subwoofers and reverb, are great when used in moderation—not so much when used to over-the-top levels. There's also a concern regarding epileptic guests and the potential for strobe lights to trigger seizures; make sure, if using a strobe light, you post warnings and notify your event's host, as well.

- *Refractors and I-Lighting.* Refraction lighting—also called "moonflowers"—are the first step to a more entertaining light show, as opposed to the utility function of par cans and strobes. Refractors include lights like digital mirror beams, disco balls, and faux-laser beams. Refractors, at their simplest, can be very useful—and in more complicated systems, these can be automatically controlled to do really cool these; these are called "intelligent" lighting, or I-Lighting, and can be the centerpiece for an array of beautiful effects. Refractors & I-Lighting are heavy, and generally considered high maintenance because of the multiple mirrored elements. They're more expensive, in their more complicated variations, than either strobes or par cans, and will almost always require DMX compatibility (more on this in a second).

Controllers

Some lighting systems are automatically controlled through built-in dimmer systems, while most professional systems require Digital Multiplex, or DMX, control. DMX control is generally done over standard XLR cables, and requires precise addressing of your lighting and dimmer packs. Your DMX controller then controls the dimmer, either manually or automatically in a sequence you program. DMX can be challenging to learn, and it's not always necessary to have a DMX-controlled system. However, the initial investment in a good DMX system will allow for future expandability.

Aside from the lights and dimmers, your lighting system will require a control board. These can be as small and light or heavy and complex as you want—and it's up to you and your budget as to what you feel is best for your system. DMX control boards can cost from under $100 to over $10,000, depending on their complexity and the programming abilities they offer. The most basic DMX consoles will simply allow control over a set of par cans; a more complicated DMX system will let you control multiple variables of complex intelligent lighting systems.

DMX control replaces the original lighting protocol, which was called 0-10V. While still commonly used in the construction trade, it's rare to see these systems used for a stage light show. They're heavy and less reliable, but you might still see some of these systems in the field; and, at the absolute cheapest level, some pre-packaged DJ systems are still run using a variant of this technology. 0-10V was a basic analog system which controlled lighting by manually varying the voltage; DMX, in comparison, uses digital translation to talk to a dimmer pack, which controls the actual voltage and passes information to the lights themselves.

Building Your Lighting Rig

Once you've decided on which pieces you'd like (and can afford) for lights, it's time to start designing your system. There are three things you need to keep in mind when you're building your lighting system:

- *Mounting.* As a mobile DJ, you'll need to be, well, mobile. Mounts can range from elaborate truss systems to simple lighting stands; I tend to appreciate a less-is-more approach, and many professional DJs I spoke with said the same. Faux-trusses and unprofessional mounting (along with most do-it-yourself projects) all look bad, but there's also one important thing to remember: safety. Your lights need to be mounted as securely as possible, and without the ability to fall over easily. Most importantly, the guests at the event you're DJing need to be able to dance the night away without having a set of par cans coming down on their heads.

- *Programming.* Controlling your lights can be very easy; some semi-pro lights have automation functions, and many have beat-sensing technology that matches the lights flashing with the beat. While considered shamefully cheesy in professional stage productions, these general-purpose automatically controlled lights aren't such a bad thing in a mobile DJ setup if you have no other option. If your lights require a DMX compatibility, you'll need to purchase either a DMX controller or dimmer pack.

- *Fog and Haze.* Fog is one of those effects that a lot of DJs (and stage lighting techs) feel the need to use. Sure, it is fun, but laying down fog on the dance floor can be both a safety hazard and an environmental nuisance. If you do decide to use intelligent lights, a light haze might be fine and appropriate to make the effects stand out; however, don't ever use oil-based hazers. While you'll find them occasionally on sale cheaply, only use water-based hazers. Oil-based haze tends to leave a disgusting film on people and objects—and you don't want your client to be embarrassed by the mess you've left.

10

We've talked about the many reasons why you, as a DJ, are in a perfect position to serve a large number of clients. The number one reason why you're the top choice for their entertainment dollar is simple: Although live bands offer a great experience and quality entertainment, they simply can't match the variety that a DJ can stuff into a small package. And that package is getting smaller and more efficient by the day, thanks to digital storage.

Just a few years ago, even the most technologically advanced small DJ services were carrying around physical CDs. That limited them to several thousand songs, at most, depending on the available space and their willingness to cart around crates of CDs. Now think about this: When was the last time you bought a physical, old-fashioned CD? Digital music storage is where it's at, both for professionals like yourself and for regular people maintaining their own collection at home.

Digital Media Storage Basics

A few years ago, storing music on CDs was the top choice for most professional DJs. A single CD holds seventy-four to eighty minutes of audio data, roughly twelve to fifteen songs; digital storage—including flash memory and hard drives—can hold up to five hundred songs per gigabyte of storage space, depending on compression and song length. And as you know, those gigabytes of portable storage are tiny—with flash memory being many times smaller than a physical CD!

In this chapter, we're going to focus on the care, maintenance, and compilation of the song lists that you use as a DJ. Your song list is your bread-and-butter—and without an updated song list, you're going to be hard-pressed to maintain a solid clientele base. Making—and maintaining—your song list is one of the most vital and potentially time-consuming activities of running a new DJ business.

Popular Song Choices

Now let's dig into that song list.

Like many members of the service industry community, you're probably going to go into your new business highly prepared but still asking yourself one question: Why can't I read my customers' minds? Being the essential DJ to your clients is going to require a great deal of guesswork—and I'll just go ahead and say it here for our own sanity: You're not going to make everybody happy. That being said, you should aim to keep a good, wide selection of music available through your DJ service.

When you're thinking about becoming a DJ service, your song list is the absolute heart of your operation. Whether you're looking to become a wedding DJ or a private event DJ, you're going to have to have a wide variety of music—mainly hits and classics—to make people happy. That's why you, as a DJ, are such a great value when compared with other forms of entertainment—you bring variety to the table.

Making choices on the songs that you carry as a DJ should be easy—with digital storage, you've got the green light to store just about everything you could possibly want within a small form factor. You should have absolutely no problem when it comes to making choices—and organizing all of this data, rather than making exclusionary choices, should be your top priority.

When starting to select songs for your playlist, you should ask yourself a few questions before dedicating storage space and easy accessibility to songs.

- *Are the new songs you're choosing up-to-date?* Listen, I love early '90s grunge rock as much as the next guy (assuming that guy also grew up in the early '90s), but your average wedding clients won't care about your awesome collection if the songs are not the standard hits they expect.
- *Are you prepared to play older classics as well as current Top 40 hits?* Remember that variety is the spice of life—and the bread-and-butter of a DJ service. Most DJs start off with classics and slowly transition to Top 40 hits while constantly monitoring who's dancing (and who's sitting down)

to make tweaks along the way. Being able to cover all of your bases is extremely important.

- *How's the quality?* Before dedicating space to songs, make sure the recording and encoding of the individual songs are up to par. A lot of low-bitrate MP3s are floating around; you want to avoid them.

Spanning the Generation Gap

When you are looking out over a difficult crowd at an event, the idea of trying to make everyone happy can feel overwhelming. One DJ offered some valuable advice: "I always try to assess the crowd and tailor my playlists based on the average age of people in the room. I go with a simple formula: My playlist reflects music that was on the charts when the majority of the customers were between eighteen and twenty-five years old; this almost-foolproof formula most always keeps people happy, even when I'm walking into a gig completely blind." Some great advice—but keep in mind your clients. If you've got a lot of 'tween birthdays, bar mitzvahs, and school dances, you'll need to tap into what's hot in that demographic, too.

Keeping Up-to-Date—You and the Charts

Although having a great selection of the classics is absolutely essential, the music industry is constantly changing. The only constant in the music industry is that consumers' tastes—and thus where they spend their money—are constantly changing. The formula for making a number one single changes every day, and nobody knows where that magic formula might come from. One day the latest boy band may be at the top of the charts; the next day, it's a cutting-edge country group. Your clients will expect you, as a DJ, to have a dynamically changing selection of songs that reflects the hits of both yesteryear and today. It's all about variety. And just like the restaurant industry, you've got a lot of pressure to stay one step ahead of your clients' requests.

Staying up-to-date with the popular charts isn't as hard as it looks. Being up-to-date first requires an intimate knowledge of the *Billboard* charts—and the *Billboard* charts will be your best friend as your DJ career continues. Let's talk more about said charts and how they affect your business.

We all know a radio hit that we love. And chances are it's on the *Billboard* charts. The *Billboard* charts come courtesy of the industry's most legendary publication, *Billboard Magazine*. *Billboard* charts are the number one, industry-standard way that songs' popularity is measured, and chances are that after a song hits the *Billboard* charts, you're going to need to know about it. Your clients will be requesting songs from the *Billboard* charts, regardless of how current the songs are—and historical *Billboard* charts will be your greatest ally in sourcing specific playlists for certain demographics. *Billboard* has several options for charts—and they're all important. None, however, is as important as the *Billboard* Hot 100.

The first chart you should hit hard is the *Billboard* Hot 100. The Hot 100 is the top

Who Decides the Hits?

According to *Billboard,* prior to 1991, all of the chart-selection processes were manual, with radio station DJs filling out reports, which were averaged to create the Top Song lists. This system generally worked, but also—according to legend—made way for some good, old-fashioned payola when it came to who ascended the charts fastest. Now, Billboard uses automated data courtesy of Nielsen Soundscan, an automatic sales- and play-tracking database, taking the guesswork (and potential bribery) out of the system.

end of *Billboard's* charts, and it contains your key to keeping updated. The Hot 100 is published weekly on Thursdays and is available, free, for public consumption at www.billboard.com. The Hot 100 is a compilation of the—you guessed it—hottest one hundred singles on all of *Billboard's* charts, compiled into one list. The Hot 100 is where you'll find the hits of today—and stay one step ahead of the hits of tomorrow. Depending on your clients, you may be playing all Hot 100 songs or none at all—every gig is different—but having access and staying up-to-date on the Hot 100 are the first way to make sure you're prepared to service the largest number of clients.

Sourcing Your Songs

Depending on whom you talk to, music downloading has either revolutionized the music industry or killed it completely. There are two schools of thought about MP3 compression and how the easy, compact, and fast transfer of song files has helped or hindered the commercial end of producing music. That being said, there's still an industry based on the production, promotion, and sale of music—and it's a big one. According to the RIAA (Recording Industry Association of America), physical sales of music dropped 6.8 percent from 2009 to 2010. That sales figure wasn't completely lost by the music industry—there was a 6 percent increase in digital download sales, from 41 percent of all sales to 47 percent. That being said, overall, year after year, the industry has lost about 10 percent of its value due to piracy. Piracy isn't an issue for just twenty-somethings filling their iPods from a BitTorrent site—it's an even bigger issue for a business like yours.

Although it's tempting for you as a DJ business to pirate all of your songs—and you're probably going to do so, even after my minilecture to the contrary—buying your songs is a really good idea for multiple reasons, the ethics of compensating the artists that have recorded the material you wish to use being one of the biggest.

About Audio Bitrates

As we start talking more about audio files, you will undoubtedly hear the word "bitrate." Bitrate is how the quality of your song files are decided. Low-bitrate compression, such as 128K MP3, gets the job done—the transmission of a long audio program as a small file—but it compromises the quality greatly. When audio is compressed into small formats such as MP3, information in the extremes of frequency range are chopped off. And, if it's a non-variable bitrate, that chopping is done without any regard for how much material is being affected. If you're using variable bitrate compression—usually 192K to 256K variable—the compression will actively listen for large amounts of information in usually cut areas. This produces a recording which compresses areas selectively to allow most of the original file to be left intact. If using MP3 compression, always look for high bitrate song files, which use variable bitrate compression.

Although the industry-standard price of 99 cents per song may seem like a lot, when buying in bulk, you'll have massive cost savings per song and per album. After all, you're not buying and storing full albums—you want just the hits, spread out over a wide variety of genres and time frames. And, even if it's inexpensive to purchase the music outright, downloading illegally will likely be the easiest way to source these songs. Most DJs download their songs in "packs"—large compilations that give them access to hits across multiple genres and for multiple purposes. Finding those packs for free can be exhilarating—until you realize that, through multiple uploads, downloads, and reassembly by torrent clients—you may not be getting the best quality possible. You could end up with corrupted songs of questionable provenance and of varying bitrates, something you should avoid for quality and consistency.

Piracy should be avoided not only because it's wrong (and costs hard-working artists and producers the money they're working for) but also because, as a small business, you already have a legal target drawn on your chest. Being caught operating with pirated material isn't good—and can lead to an uncomfortable fine or worse. Although the chances of that happening are remote, you owe it to yourself and your clients to keep yourself on the right side of the law.

DJ supply services such as Promo Only (www.promoonly.com) tend to work on a subscription basis. Once a month you receive a packet of CDs containing digital files—of proven quality—of the latest hits. This arrangement keeps you constantly updated but does come at a price—one that changes frequently, depending on the costs involved in licensing the material. However, you're guaranteed that your material—be it Hot 100 or a playlist of legacy songs—will be of high quality.

Sourcing legacy songs is a lot easier than it might sound but involves a much more significant investment of time and storage space. Although you've probably got a great idea of the songs you want to have in your arsenal, a lot of DJ supply services—more on these in the next section—will gladly get you sourced in full for a price. Promo Only received the highest feedback from the vast majority of DJs I spoke with. We'll talk more about Promo Only in just a minute.

FLAC versus MP3

In the audio world, MP3 is the absolute king of the portable audio file formats. MP3 compression has come a long way since it made its first public appearance in the mid- to late-1990s. In fact, I still remember the first MP3 I downloaded—a washy, tightly compressed MP3 of R.E.M.'s "Losing My Religion." It sounded terrible, but I remember being blown away that I could download one whole song in less than twenty minutes! And the quality—and the popularity of using MP3s—has grown ever since.

As we talked about previously, the quality of your music depends directly upon the quality of your files. This is why lower-bitrate, low-quality MP3 files tend to have a washy-sounding high end (think vocal sibilance and cymbal crashes being cut short sonically) and less-than-solid low-frequency response. Low-quality MP3s are your biggest enemy in achieving sonic perfection during your performances. That's why sourcing your MP3 files from a reputable stock house is a big priority.

Aside from MP3 compression, there's been a big move to using uncompressed, unaltered audio files in the DJ world. That's because bigger file sizes can be easily transferred via today's high-speed Internet, and there's also easy capability (and the cheap storage necessary) to rip uncompressed files from CD. There's also the movement toward what's called *lossless compression,* which is a lightly compressed file transfer format that many audio engineers prefer over MP3. FLAC and SHN files (the two most common lossless mediums) generally compress an audio file by 25 percent and offer full, uncompressed quality. The problem is that FLAC and SHN formats are generally only for portability—they're hard for some playback mediums to handle and generally require conversion to WAV or AIF format for playback. You'll want to be careful with your storage space, and high-bitrate, variable-pass MP3 files will give you 99 percent of the sonic quality of a FLAC file to most people's ears.

The file format you choose to store your music in is up to you and your budget for digital storage. FLAC will always give higher quality but at a premium cost for additional storage. Many compression schemes, such as Apple's Lossless Audio Codec, are also offering ultra-high resolution using selective compression; however, cross-compatibility is an issue. Unless you plan on only using one brand of device, it's best to stick to a more widespread format.

Serving Unique Demographics

Although the Hot 100 and legacy playlists you're selecting service the vast majority of your clientele, you should also be prepared to serve the varied demographics that make any city a diverse, exciting place. Many of your clients may request a standard playlist built around pop hits; others may request specific hits from their religious or cultural background. Servicing these populations is yet another way that your DJ business can stand out from the competition—and although it may be more

Let's do some brainstorming. What demographics in your area might you be able to serve—
and thus increase your customer base? The answer should help you in planning your song lists
(and in the scripts you learn to follow along with):

Religious groups:

_____

_____

_____

_____

_____

Ethnic groups:

_____

_____

_____

_____

_____

Cultural institutions (fraternal organizations, colleges, service organizations):

_____

_____

_____

_____

_____

Local traditions:

_____

_____

_____

_____

_____

difficult for you to break into a market whose culture you don't fully understand, it's at least worth an effort to have access to and a moderate understanding of the complexities that come with more diverse demographics.

In some areas, ethnic clientele might make up a vast majority of your business. Many areas have high concentrations of diverse ethnic populations—and they're ripe for the picking for your DJ business. Keeping yourself open and sensitive to the needs of the local ethnic communities will help you pick up more work and a more diverse client base.

11

Being an Emcee

Anybody who's been to a lot of weddings knows what it's like when the DJ who's working the event isn't playing with a full deck. Erratic song choices, cheesy showmanship: Most likely the person you're picturing right now is wearing a cheap, disheveled tuxedo that's a few weddings past needing a dry cleaning. You don't want to be that DJ.

Being a good emcee—the word is longhand for the abbreviation *MC* for "master of ceremonies"—is sometimes going to be the most trying part of your job. Despite the inconvenience of loading in heavy equipment, dealing with the requests of the public, and maintaining the behind-the-scenes tasks of your business, you might find this role of entertainer to be absolutely exhausting. Many of the DJs I spoke to told me that frequently their emcee duties drive them nuts. But, as every one of them quickly reminded me, there's nothing more rewarding than a night when everything goes right.

In this chapter, we're going to talk about your job as an entertainer, after the songs are chosen and the equipment is ready to go.

Basics of Showmanship

Being a good DJ for any event requires you to be outgoing, friendly, and accommodating. I know, that already sounds like you, right? Well, keep in mind that not everybody is the outgoing type and that not everybody is the first person to jump onto the dance floor. That very reason is why you as a DJ exist: You're going to get that person who isn't having fun to get off his butt, get onto the dance floor, and have a great time. That's what your clients are paying you for: It's not just the music they're after; they want you to create the entertainment, too.

Although all good DJs recognize that the true value of their work comes from the fact that they offer a great variety of musical entertainment, they also entertain the crowd and make sure that everyone has a good time. That's not easy. We know what it's like to deal with friends and family who are stubborn, and it's even more exhausting when there's no emotional connection to the people you're dealing with. That being said, being a good DJ is just as much about having fun yourself—and showing it proudly—as it is about making others have a good time. If the DJ is being lively and enjoying the event, chances are the crowd will, too. Likewise, if you're DJing an event where the client asks you to lie low and simply provide some soothing background music, you should avoid playing the part of showman and honor the request.

Whenever you book an event, you need to follow a lot of steps so you can tailor your DJ act to the client's exact needs:

- *Determine your client's perfect vision.* Ask your client exactly what she wants your role to be. She might want you to run the entire evening, which is most common at wedding receptions. She might also ask you to simply play background music for an event and make the song selections as seamless as possible. It's up to your client. Ask her specifically what she wants from you and make sure you feel comfortable that you can deliver what she asks for.
- *Know when to tone it down.* A wedding or other event that has a large number of older, less-agile guests won't appreciate your trying to get everyone to do the Cha Cha Slide. Make sure that your shtick meets your crowd's energy level.
- *Understand your role and stick to it.* Make sure that, after you define your role with your clients, you stick to it.

Drugs and Alcohol on the Job

One of the worst problems I see in the music industry is the disgraceful number of good musicians and DJs who succumb to the easy accessibility of drugs and alcohol while working. When you're working as a mobile DJ, you've got a lot more liability than some musician who's just on stage for an hour or two and then off to the bar; you're hauling equipment and managing the flow of the evening's entertainment, and you've got a lot of things to balance at once. Your clients do not deserve an intoxicated DJ—they're paying for you to put on the best show possible.

Alcohol will be served at many of the events you work, and generally, as a working member of the event, you'll have access to it. Drinking heavily on the job is frowned upon at every other job in the world—so why is yours any different just because you're having fun at a party while working? Many clients will specifically request that you not drink, but some will feel obligated to let you in on the open bar action. It's a nice gesture, but it's a privilege that you can easily abuse.

Being drunk or high on the job is seriously dangerous when you're in control of as many elements as you are when DJing. You're controlling high-volume-producing audio equipment—a slip of technique is all it takes to create deafening feedback, causing hearing loss. You could damage your own equipment, blowing a speaker and causing expensive downtime. The possibilities for drunken slip-ups are numerous—not to mention the fact that, as we all know, the things you say on the mic may not sound nearly as cute to the other people in the room as they do to you. Being in control of this much at once is sometimes difficult when sober, let alone drunk.

Drugs, also, should never be an option while working as a professional DJ. Aside from the fact that showing up high to a paid event is completely classless on your part, the embarrassment for both you and your clients would be profound if your drugs or drug use were discovered by the event staff. Stay clean and be as sharp and alert as your clients deserve. What you do off the clock is your own business, but keep things on the up-and-up when you're with clients. They'll appreciate it and show you that appreciation with repeat and referral business.

Emcee Etiquette 101

Being a good emcee is about making people feel comfortable, engaged in the entertainment, and happy to be at the event. You also are responsible, depending on your degree of involvement, for planning the flow of the evening's special events and

Emcee Empathy

When you're developing your stage show as an emcee, think about the times when you've been picked out of a crowd and made to feel uncomfortable. That's the kind of power you'll have over people during events like weddings and dances, where you'll be in control of the flow of the evening's festivities.

entertainment. There's a lot of power in being in control of the entertainment on the dance floor.

Being extra sensitive to your clients and their friends and family is of the utmost importance—and having fun and being able to laugh at yourself aren't such bad things, either. Keep in mind a few suggestions when you're behind the mic:

- *Display sensitivity.* Don't force people into the action if they look uncomfortable. Don't point out people for their flaws; even if you overhear someone in the event planner's group make a joke or use a funny nickname for a person, repeating it in public can upset someone.
- *Stay away from race, religion, and disabilities.* Never, ever go into territory that can hurt someone's feelings and affect his or her civil liberties. Never.
- *Remember key people.* Not introducing the father of the bride properly—especially if he's paying for the wedding and your services—can be an instant way to cost yourself a lot of word-of-mouth. Mispronouncing names, forgetting who's who, and deviating from the script that you and the event planner have come up with are extremely likely to cost you business.

Dress and Appearance

Part of the reason you're being hired as a professional DJ is that you're supposed to be a professional—and being professional isn't just about the songs you pick and how great your equipment is. Part of true professionalism is how you come across to your clients via your dress and your appearance when you show up to a gig. What you wear largely will depend on the type of event you're DJing—you want to fit into the event, but you absolutely do not want to stylistically upstage the key people in the event. As in many other jobs in the service industry, you're going to be representing both the customers you're hired to work for and your business. Showing up dressed inappropriately for an event is a good way to make sure you won't be asked back (or recommended).

Here are a few tips to remember about your dress and appearance as a professional DJ:

- *A tuxedo is a bad idea.* The stereotypical bad wedding DJ whom we talked about earlier generally shows up in a tux that's in need of a trip to the dry cleaner. There's another reason why you should not wear a tux: If worn at all, tuxedos should be reserved for the top tier of the wedding party; that's not you. If tuxedos are being worn at all, it's not going to look good if you, the groom, and the man of honor all dress the same. Just think about this: If you're a female DJ, and you show up to the wedding in a wedding dress, how would that look?

- *Always ask first.* Your event may have a casual theme or a beach theme; make sure you're ready to dress appropriately to blend in as if you were an invited guest. You don't need your dress to call attention to you—and you certainly don't want to offend your clients. Asking your clients what they'd prefer you do about dress is a must. Your clients will be the ones signing your paycheck, so it's only natural that they call the shots.

- *Avoid common social mistakes.* Don't show up smelling bad, don't show up drunk or high, and don't take frequent smoke breaks if you're a smoker—in fact, find a way to avoid the craving completely. Interacting with the wedding party or event planners when you've been drinking alcohol, using drugs, or smelling of either is extremely bad judgment.

- *Mind the photographer.* Remember that if you're DJing a wedding, the event will be photographed in great detail. You're going to make it into some of the photos—and it's going to be bad if you look terrible when those photos come back to the client. Don't put yourself in that position!

Scripts and Rehearsal

Part of being a performer—be it a musician, poet, or dancer—is rehearsing. Rehearsal is the least-fun part of any performing art, and many artists I know find absolutely any excuse to avoid rehearsing. I've also seen a great number of bands have absolute breakup-level meltdowns because of the stress that rehearsing brings—and as a DJ, you're unfortunately not exempt from rehearsing, either.

By this point, it's pretty clear to you that your clients call all of the shots. For most events—especially weddings—you'll have a script that the couple wishes you use to help move along the events of the evening. You'll generally need to be on the same page about introductions, dinner and drink announcements, and how the night's entertainment should go.

After you and the client agree on a script and timeline, you'll most likely be asked to attend a rehearsal for your event. This could be a long rehearsal or a quick pre-event meeting, and you'll learn the basics that the client wants you to know. Every wedding, dance, and other event is going to be unique—and although you'll need to know a few key items to make the evening flow successfully, you'll mainly be at the beck and call of your client and what he or she wishes.

When formulating your event playbook, you should ask a few questions of your client at or before your first rehearsal or planning meeting. See pages 120–21 for a simple worksheet for you to fill out. It'll help you organize your thought process for your upcoming event.

Dealing with Requests

Requests are one of the things that make you, as a DJ, a very valuable commodity. Normally, DJs in music clubs aren't there to take requests—they've got their sets, and they're sticking to them. Requesting songs in that environment is usually considered greatly unfashionable. Most of your events, however, will be the perfect setting for a lot of guest requests, and it's up to you to handle them gracefully.

There are a few rules for dealing with requests, and there are also a few things you might want to consider when it comes to the ethics of requests; you might not think about it now, but when you're in the middle of a party and you're being faced with some tough decisions, you'll be glad you had a plan.

Requests can come in all shapes and sizes; that's why having a long song list is really important. But just having a song doesn't mean you should play it—keep a few rules in mind when dealing with requests from your event's guests:

- *Know your boss.* Don't play something that your hosts would find offensive. If they've requested a mostly country playlist, don't offend their tastes by playing a request for heavy metal. Make sure that someone's request fits the aesthetic of the event. If it doesn't, politely decline saying that the event's hosts requested a specific playlist.
- *Accepting tips is optional.* Many people will try to tip for their opportunity to have their request played, and it's up to you and how you feel about the issue as to whether that's appropriate. Many DJs will ask the event's organizers first—they will tell you if they think accepting gratuities is appropriate. You can also offer, as part of your business, to accept tips on behalf of your event's sponsors—a charitable donation for a private organization or honeymoon spending cash for a wedding couple—it may feel like you're passing up a good money making opportunity, but the goodwill

Ask your client the following questions and use the answers to create your event playbook.

What music do you want played for an introduction?

_____
_____
_____
_____

Dinner music/cocktail music (before the dance party starts)?

_____
_____
_____
_____

Announcements pre-event?

_____
_____
_____
_____

How to introduce key people (if at all)?

_____
_____
_____
_____

What specific group dances do you want worked into the event?

_____
_____
_____
_____

Any specific songs you wish to include?

_____
_____
_____
_____

Any dedications or special requests?

_____

_____

_____

_____

How do you want the night to be paced?

_____

_____

_____

_____

Anything you do *not* want played?

_____

_____

_____

_____

How do you want the evening to end?

_____

_____

_____

_____

At what time, promptly, is the event over?

_____

_____

_____

_____

your customers feel from such a gesture is worth much, much more than a hundred bucks in tips.

- *Be organized.* There are a few electronic DJ request systems out there (such as SoftJock's Remote Request software—which uses a computer to index requests from the public, available at www.softjock.com), and they're great for being organized. You can also do the old-fashioned pen-and-paper method; whatever your way of dealing with it, make sure you stay organized. You never know when you'll get a ton of requests at once.

Crowd requests can be fun, but they can also give you a market advantage: Keeping track of your requests is a great idea, as it can give a lot of insight into the tastes of different demographics. Keeping notes on what's getting hot in music by way of crowd requests can help you play these songs more often—and make more people happier.

Crowd Control

As the event DJ, it's not necessarily your job to be the bouncer for the event. There should be, if necessary, external security there to handle these types of issues. However, as the most visible person (other than the bartender) at any type of party or event, you might be called upon to either assist in removing troublesome guests or be asked to help in controlling crowd issues. You're also at one distinct advantage to anyone else in the room: you've got the sound system, and you have a microphone. That's going to make you capable of making announcements, cutting off music, and turning on the lights if necessary. You're going to be the one in charge of how the entertainment and ambience of the event are controlled, and you might have to restore things to more of a "normal" situation if something bad happens.

Making Announcements

We've talked about not being too invasive with your announcements, but keep in mind you might have to use your announcement-making abilities to get people's attention in the case of an emergency. Always be aware and always be prepared to make an announcement if you need to.

Sometimes, you'll come across guests at these events that have had a bit too much to drink and decide it's time to act inappropriately. As the DJ, you'll likely be the one to experience this happening in realtime while watching the dance floor. You should be comfortable using your authority as the DJ to let the guest know they need to take a step back.

What's the best way to deal with a problem guest? Here's a quick checklist to keep in mind:

- *Ask nicely first.* If you believe someone's behavior is becoming erratic or dangerous, ask them nicely to calm down. You might also wish to confer with the event's bartender to ask how much that guest has had to drink, and possibly let the bartender use his or her authority to cut off the guest's alcohol consumption.
- *If asking fails, request to speak to the event's host.* Ask to speak to them in private, and ask their opinion on how to deal with the problem. This may include you having to make a decision on having this guest removed; that's why it's good to have external security on site. Usually, a verbal warning from the event's host is enough to keep anyone in line.
- *Never, ever use or participate in violence.* If a guest gets out of control, you should never feel all right putting your hands on them. Keep yourself at a distance, and avoid getting involved in any kind of physical altercation. If anything ever becomes physical, back away from the situation and immediately call the police.

12 | The Wedding Industry

Three hundred billion dollars. That's what the wedding industry is projected to be worth in the year 2012, according to the Simmons Survey. That's a ton of money—and there's a lot of it with your name on it.

Ask any self-employed DJs what keeps them busiest, and chances are they'll tell you that weddings supply the majority of their business. It's no secret that weddings are some of the most elaborate and costly events known to humanity, and as any recently married person will tell you, a wide variety of expenditures is necessary to put on the perfect wedding day. As a DJ trying to be the top in your field, you're going to have to compete for a few of those dollars.

The average "original budget"—meaning the minimum that a couple commits for a wedding—was, in 2011, according to the Association for Wedding Professionals International, an astounding $20,000. That's before you add the costs of engagement and wedding rings, venue fees, catering, favors, and, of course, the entertainment.

Who's Signing Your Paycheck?

According to *Brides Magazine* in 2011, 30 percent of most married couples paid for the whole wedding themselves. Only 17 percent of couples followed the tradition of the bride's parents paying for the wedding, with 53 percent of couples financing their wedding through a variety of means, including personal loans and credit cards.

There's a lot of competition out there, and just like every other DJ on Earth, you'll be making your best paychecks courtesy of the wedding industry. In this chapter, we'll conduct a crash course in the wedding industry. You'll learn the basics of this always-changing market. Remember that tastes change rapidly and that nowhere else is this fact more evident than the wedding DJ market. Being on top in this game requires a dedication to being the best, and the competition is fierce. But armed with as much knowledge as possible, you'll be on your way to being a superstar wedding DJ.

Understanding the Wedding Industry—And Your Role in It

Nowhere, other than Disneyland, is creating the ultimate fantasy world more important than within the wedding industry. So, serving the wedding industry takes finesse and attention to detail that aren't always necessary for a commercial DJ. When doing a commercial gig, you've got a lot less structure, a lot more latitude to perform whatever music you see fit, and a much more relaxed environment. Weddings, on the other hand, aren't so flexible—and again, there are always exceptions. That's why you, as a DJ, will generally command a higher price for your wedding performances than you would for a corporate or private event. That's just the nature of the wedding industry—due to higher demand and the stricter demands that most couples have, everybody from caterers to DJs to jewelers raises prices accordingly.

The wedding industry wasn't always the behemoth that it is today. Not until after World War II did weddings became a big deal in America. Prior to that, large weddings with commercial venues were the folly of the wealthy. Most weddings took place at the home, with receptions being centered around a community

A Frilly Fact

During World War II, many materials were rationed or restricted—including the pure white lace that many brides used to create a traditional wedding dress. The largest dress makers in the country were so alarmed that they couldn't produce their products that they campaigned the government to allow a waiver on lace rationing—on the argument that traditional weddings boosted morale. They won.

potluck-style dinner, with friends and family supplying the food. Weddings were a simple, community-oriented affair that didn't necessarily cost a lot of money. Many happy marriages began in the bride's parents' living room.

With prosperous postwar times came the middle class, and with the middle class came the dream of upper-class weddings. At a time when suburban American culture was quickly becoming more homogenized, weddings, too, became a staple of the American suburban existence. As salaries grew and resources became more plentiful, weddings became something that even those of modest means could afford—and not just a living-room wedding like their parents likely had.

And that is why the wedding industry generates a ton of money every year for vendors like yourself. Aside from catering, alcohol, and venue rental, your services as an entertainer are likely to be one of the first items a newly engaged couple budgets for. As we've talked about, DJs are the number one choice for wedding entertainment for many reasons. The average wedding's expenditure on entertainment is 10 to 15 percent of the budget: around $2,500 on a $25,000 wedding. Of course, that figure can be higher or lower, depending on the couple, their budget, and the requirements of the event.

In order to understand the wedding industry, you have to understand the thinking within the planning stages of a wedding event; you're there to help the couple create the perfect celebration, and the right entertainment is a part of every vision. You're being trusted to create the sonic blueprint of the evening, which can make or break the evening. It's why having a long, varied song list is extremely important—and why patience, appearance, and demeanor are exceptionally important as well.

How Trends Change

Before we dig deeper, a quick note about trends. Weddings are, like any other service industry events, completely dependent on the whims of the people signing the paycheck. And most couples—regardless of the budget they've set aside—want the most modern, sleekest wedding that reflects the current style as best it can. As an event professional, you're going to get a lot of varied requests from your customers, but most of the time, your wedding customers will simply expect that you'll be up-to-date with your song list, appearance, and stage show. They'll expect your equipment to be in top-notch shape and your entire performance to be as unobtrusive as possible. There's a saying that "class never goes out of style," and that's certainly something you as a DJ should remember.

Over time, you'll find that your wedding clients change when it comes to their needs and expectations. That's just a natural part of the evolution of anything, and you'll need to find a way to keep up. Whether it's keeping a keen eye on the wedding industry publications you can find on any magazine rack or frequenting wedding planning forums online, it's important to be on top of trends. Being able to meet and exceed client expectations, even in such a dynamic industry, is extremely important.

Trends in the wedding industry tend to follow popular culture, especially royal weddings. Take, for example, the marriage of Prince William of the British royal family. Many of the wedding DJs I spoke with were inundated with requests for "royal weddings on a budget," with many brides copying the Princess Catherine look and style for their own weddings. By staying on top of current wedding trends, you'll be well-positioned to take a large share of your local market.

How Can You Keep Up-to-Date in Wedding Trends?

- *Always stay informed.* The best wedding professionals know the trends and have no problem replicating them on demand. Online publications like *Veil Magazine* and *The Knot* can be helpful.
- *Talk to your clients.* The best thing you can do is listen to your customers; they'll guide you in the right direction. Trends are important only if your clients try to follow them.
- *Prune your playlist.* Although I don't ever advocate deleting songs—you never know when someone will absolutely demand to hear a one-hit wonder's obscure 90s song that you've thrown into the circular file—it's not necessary to keep the same playlists year after year. Make sure you're playing a lot of current hits alongside the standards.

Regional Trends in Weddings

Aside from popular culture's influence on the song selection at weddings, you'll find that your regional location helps determine what your customers demand. Although there's no hard-and-fast rule about the geographical boundaries between areas that prefer specific musical genres, you can apply a few generic tips if you're going to be serving a diverse geographic area.

Understanding regional expectations is important, and they are always changing. Often the best advice that I can give is that you'll get the answers you need by talking to your clients. Understanding the regional variations in tastes will require your knowing what your clients expect, and that's going to change yearly.

Another important fact to understand is that many popular songs have regional variations; in some parts of the country, when a DJ is asked to play the "Electric Slide," that means the Grandmaster Slice version of the song; in the southern United States, if you play anything other than the 1986 version by Marcia Griffiths, you're going to end up with an empty dance floor. The same goes for songs such as "Cotton-Eyed Joe" (Isaac Peyton Sweat's version is a southern staple; the Rednex remix is more popular elsewhere) and the "Cha Cha Slide" (several versions of this song are making the rounds; it's mostly popular in the northern United States). Being prepared and making sure that any special requests are honored to avoid disappointment by your client are important.

Apart from regional variations, it's important to understand the religious and cultural makeup of your local customers. It might surprise you to find out that most couples who do choose to have a wedding large enough to justify the expenditure of a DJ are couples who have strong religious beliefs. Although many nonreligious couples have large weddings every year, you'll find that a slight majority of your customers do practice a faith and that in some regions, ethnic religions are extremely concentrated. Most of my wedding DJ friends in the New York City area perform at a large number of Jewish events and have to tailor their events to match. In the Detroit area, a majority of the ethnic population is Muslim, and the DJs there typically provide diverse playlists that include American Top 40 and Muslim traditional celebration songs. Religious customs—especially at Jewish and Muslim-themed events—require a lot more specialized playlist than do other events.

Complete preparedness is the number one goal that you as a DJ should strive for, and understanding your local customs is extremely important. Although the regional variations around the world are too vast to name here individually, always take time to become keenly aware of what's "hot" in your local community. You might be surprised by what you'll find—and you never know: You may find a way to edge out your competition by serving an under-served population.

Weddings: Know Your Customers

As we talked about in the beginning of this chapter, the standard American wedding is ever-changing. In my grandparents' time, a simple home wedding was the gold standard for anybody outside the upper class; in those times, a lavish wedding with a reception including entertainment and a catered meal was possible only for the upper class. As time went on and post–World War II prosperity transformed the nation (and etched out a middle class), commercial wedding venues became much more important, and with them, the role of entertainment professionals such as yourself grew exponentially and continues to do so.

In those early days of postwar prosperity, many of our wedding traditions as we know them today were born. Elements such as invitation styles, engagement rings, wedding dresses, and other major (and minor) details of a modern wedding were all introduced to the masses when the newly minted middle class was proven to lack the social graces of the upper class; many manufacturers set the standards we use today as a way to teach upper-class wedding etiquette to the middle class in a way that was easy to replicate on a wide scale.

Still, today there are several types of weddings. The most common is still the traditional religious wedding followed by a reception, usually held either in a neighboring event space or a hall attached to the church. This type of traditional religious wedding is mainly popular in the southern and mid-southern United States. In many other areas—especially the coasts and urban northern cities—secular weddings, performed by a nondenominational officiant at a location other than a church—are becoming the more prominent theme. As a wedding DJ, you should be more than prepared to work both types of events.

Many couples also opt to have wedding-like events at various stages in their marriage, and those types of events are well worth your time as a DJ. Renewing vows and remarrying a spouse are popular events—and a common way to celebrate milestone anniversaries. Many of these events are a lot looser and a fair amount less expensive than a traditional, all-out wedding; generally, your cost to your client will be 15 to 20 percent less due to the timing and nature of the event. Still, wedding-related events like these will account for a good chunk of your private

Buying Power!

It's a fact that newly engaged and newlywed couples are hardwired to spend money; according to a *Brides Magazine* survey, new life partners, whether engaged or married, make up about 2.6 percent of the population; however, that 2.6 percent accounts for 70 percent of major household spending at any given time. That's a lot of buying power, and often it starts with spending a lot of money on a wedding!

party income when you are not DJing "real" weddings. Being able to serve these events well is an important skill to retain.

Your Level of Involvement

As all event professionals will tell you, their clients come in all shapes, sizes, and tastes. One day these professionals may be putting on a lavish sit-down dinner for two hundred, complete with champagne toast, caviar, and ice sculptures; the next day, they're organizing a wedding reception barbecue at a lakeside pavilion with a keg of beer sitting in the corner and the groom wearing his finest fishing boots. People who have money to spend and the desire to host the best party they've ever been to tend to want their personal tastes to be reflected in every aspect of the event, and they want their personality to shine through even at the cost of frustrating the event professionals they've retained. This is a dangerous stage in the game, especially in wedding events. This is where you have the highest potential to spar with your client, and it's before this stage that you should always clarify your level of involvement when DJing a wedding.

Often you will walk into a wedding event with carte blanche to do whatever you wish. You'll define the script of the reception, and the couple will work with you to rehearse how the event will go. From the introduction of the wedding party to the couple's first dance, you'll need to work with your clients to script out what they see fit for their reception, and many times, you'll need to clarify just how involved they want you to be.

Being a performer, whether a DJ or a stage musician, is all about moderation. You have to be able to do whatever the event calls for, and doing this can be a little difficult if you feel that you've fine-tuned your DJ set to something that you enjoy performing. Some clients will ask that you be boisterous and the life of the party; others will ask that you sit back and let the music play while they take the lead in entertaining the guests.

When you're meeting with your wedding clients, it's important to clarify how involved you need to be with the structure of the events. Use the "Finding Your Role in Wedding Receptions" worksheet on page 132 for important questions to ask.

Ask your wedding clients the following questions and use the answers to establish your responsibilities and level of involvement at the event.

Are you responsible for emceeing the event?

_____

Are you responsible for announcing the entrance of the parties?

_____

What announcements should you make and at what time?

_____
_____
_____
_____
_____
_____

What specific dances does the client want?

_____
_____
_____
_____
_____
_____

What time should you announce last call and last dance?

_____

How often does the client want to hear from you during the reception?

_____
_____

Should you be responsible for announcing meal times, or is this done already?

_____

How much rehearsal time does the client wish to have prior to the event?

_____

Package Deals for Weddings

As a DJ working your way through the minefield of wedding planning, you'll undoubtedly find that many of your clients are looking for the same thing we all want in anything we buy: absolute value. Although it may seem like a bargain to you, given how much time and dedication you've put into it, you'll likely find that your pricing structure will always be subject to questioning and attempted negotiation. Many DJs find it advantageous to offer their pricing in terms of full packages, rather than a la carte options, when dealing with wedding clients. This is because weddings are extremely stressful times in anyone's life; when you look at the planning that goes into just the reception, it's easy to see why most couples prefer to have details handed to them in tidy, easy-to-read packages.

When formulating how much you'll charge for a wedding client, you should keep in mind a few rules, especially when packaging your services:

- *Always offer value.* Make sure you're not packaging your services in such a way that you're taking a "take it or leave it" stance. You, as a small business person, should always be ready to unbundle your services and give the clients exactly what they need (and can afford). Be prepared with various packages to suit every situation.
- *Be prepared.* Don't undersell yourself in the production department; always make sure the clients are paying for the equipment they need, even if you're open to negotiating your services.
- *Understand your clients.* Make sure that any packages you offer don't contradict the specs already laid out by your clients. It may seem redundant, but you should never put together a package quote that you know is outside the realm of what your clients need.

13 Business Endgame

Every small business starts off with extremely big hopes. There are lots of dreams of success—and of being able to write your own ticket as a self-employed person. You've got every reason to be optimistic, too—because your success will directly reflect the hard work that you've committed to making this all happen for yourself and your DJ business. Everybody—myself included—hopes for the best for your new DJ business.

Unfortunately, life doesn't always work out the way we want. Having to close your business—for any number of the reasons a small business can fail—can be absolutely devastating. It's completely different from being fired from a job; there you lose just the income and whatever collateral benefits came from your job. If you lose your small business, you're giving up something that's become such a large part of your identity.

In this chapter, we're going to talk about your business endgame—that is, your plan of action in case the venture doesn't work out the way you wanted or in case it succeeds and expands beyond just your one-person show. Yes, failure is unfortunate and can bring a lot of heartache on you and your family, but thinking about it now and going into your business with a plan of action in case the worst happens are important.

Let's hope that you will need only the success tips—and that everything is always perfect for you. But in case the business doesn't go well, sections in this chapter are for you. They won't make it easier, but they'll certainly give you a clear idea of what happens when it's time to let the business go.

Let's look at what you should do to minimize your losses if your new DJ business fails—and get you started on a new path as quickly as possible.

> ## Small Business Failure Rates
>
> Yes, new businesses fail—and they fail frequently. According to the Small Business Administration, in ten years' time, 70 percent of small businesses will be out of business (or reformulated to open as something different). The odds are stacked against you—and it's up to you to work hard to achieve success. Sometimes, even with hard work, things don't work out. That's okay.

Your Reputation

Any small business owner knows that word-of-mouth is absolutely everything. Many successful businesses build decades-strong reputations on nothing more than a little word-of-mouth advertising and some goodwill in their community. Others have to advertise furiously and frequently on every medium possible to get people to remember they're even there. Guess which method is the first to drain a new business dry?

We talked earlier about establishing your online presence, collecting quality reviews, and making sure that every customer is as happy as he or she can be. You also remember (and likely have found out first-hand by now) that, even with your best efforts, you'll likely have customers you just can't please. Whether they misunderstood what they were signing up for or simply underestimated the time or financial commitments that a professional DJ such as yourself brings to the table, a legitimate customer complaint is bound to arise from time to time. How you handle this situation and how well you execute your plan of action are extremely important.

Reputation management firms are becoming more and more prevalent in today's Internet-driven society. Many small businesses and individuals just like you hire these firms to help erase bad Internet feedback. Unfortunately, bad Internet feedback is still, most likely, honest feedback. As we talked about earlier, you should always try to resolve any issues a client brings forward to the satisfaction of the client as best you can. That's where reputation management firms find their prey—businesses way too eager to hide truthful negative feedback.

Reputation management firms work like this: You let them know about something online that you don't like, and they go to work hiding it from the general public. Many businesses seem to think that these firms will happily find a way to delete negative reviews and keep everything online about them positive. In fact, these firms generally go to great lengths to manipulate web content and search engine optimization to hide your online reviews from the first couple of pages of search engine results. As a small business owner, you don't want this. Most importantly, the vast majority of the purpose-built online content that would replace a negative review is complete fluff. It is content that will devalue your overall standing and reputation among web-savvy consumers—potentially a large amount of your clients.

Avoid the trap of reputation management. As we talked about, when you get a bad review, the best course of action to is suck it up, admit that something went wrong (whether it was your fault or not), and work to keep your customers. Reputation is everything in any business, and it's up to you to keep yours sterling in the correct way—by providing something of high quality and good value every single time you're hired.

Unfair attacks do happen. You never know when an uncouth rival will pop up and try to bury you as a marketing tactic. This kind of behavior is for amateurs—and that's not you. Don't give in and fight fire with fire. It's best to go directly to both the source and the platform for the unfair attack. Explain why you're disappointed with the unfair and untrue post, and after you've positively determined that the negative online material isn't legitimate, go to the company that hosts the site where the review is posted, explain the situation, and work to get it removed. This won't always be easy, but it's worth pursuing if you're under attack unfairly.

Above all, remember this: Your reputation is worth everything. Do what you can to maintain it in the noblest way possible; that applies to any employees you take on, too. Anybody you hire should know exactly the standards you wish to uphold and should be able to adhere to them flawlessly.

Keeping—and Evolving—Your Standards

The most important service that any business can offer its clients is consistency— the ability to deliver a solid product every single time without fail. In a business as dynamically changing as yours, we've talked about what you'll need to do to make yourself stand out (in a good way): Stay ahead of the current trends in the DJ business, maintain a carefully pruned playlist of the standards, and be prepared to meet your clients' expectations in ways never thought necessary as time goes on. Remember that maintaining your standards can easily walk a fine line between being fresh and being stale. That's what we're going to focus on here—because becoming out-of-date is a kiss of death for most small businesses.

Think about it for a moment: Everybody knows a restaurant, bar, or other business that offers a consistent but boring, outdated, and tired product. It has been in business since before time began, and it has had legions of followers whose numbers have slowly dwindled with time—but who keep the business busy doing the same old thing, year after year. The business may have found what it does well, and it is sticking to it—to a fault. That's not what your DJ business needs to be. You should make sure that you're constantly evolving with the times and avoiding a lot of the common pitfalls of businesses who get too comfortable.

Before they kill your hard-earned small business, let's talk about some of the elements that can make your DJ business fall out of favor when compared with your potentially more trend-conscious competition.

- *How's your song list?* We talked about this in detail, and it's important that you maintain your song list with the most current hits available. Your clients will, many times, expect to hear their pop and Top 40 favorites—and you need to be able to deliver the newest and greatest on demand. Keeping up with what's hot on the *Billboard* charts will make you look like a star—and a versatile one at that.
- *How's your sound?* Again as we talked about, digital equipment and more-efficient speaker systems are revolutionizing the industry. Showing up to a gig where you're commanding a reasonable price while still hauling outdated and poor-sounding equipment is the easiest way for you to look like a bad value to your customers.
- *How's your stage show?* Being outdated and stale with your emcee skills is one of the quickest ways to lose business. Imagine getting a reputation for having decent music but a terrible emcee show—you'll lose a lot of business from your trendier customers. Keeping yourself and the way you present your show fresh and free from tackiness is the best way to keep your customers.

Expanding or Selling Your Business

After you've reached a point of success that you're happy with, you might consider expanding. It's not always the most prudent choice to make, but it sure is tempting; you might find an opportunity to buy additional equipment at a discount; you might have way more business in your local area than you can do single-handedly, and you might see an opportunity to do that. You might be tempted to expand your business for many reasons, and it's important that you think about that decision very thoroughly.

Expanding your business when it's not the right time to do so can be devastating. However, if you expand your business when you have the resources to comfortably do so, doing so is always a good investment. You have to be sure you have enough business to justify your expansion and not just on a seasonal or temporary basis—you need to be able to justify (and recoup) your investment over the long term. Expanding can be a proud step, or it can be the beginning of a lot of problems for you and your business. Make the decision carefully, and you'll likely be rewarded with a long-term career with your new DJ business. Just because you've got a solid business now doesn't mean that you will with a more expensive, larger version. Sometimes, even if you gave it your best shot, your business might not be working out for you personally. Your business might not work out for you for a lot of reasons, and you'll need to either sell your business or close its doors.

Here is one of the best situations that you could find yourself in: Your business has a steady clientele, a decent profit, and a good reputation within your community. But despite its success, it might just become too much for you to handle by yourself. If this is the case, you might want to consider selling your business to somebody who has more time to put into the effort that your business deserves. Fortunately, people are always looking for an opportunity to start their own business, and as you've learned in this book, you have to do a lot of work behind the scenes until you make a profit; many people like the proposition of walking into a moderately successful business and simply taking over operations without having to put in the heartache of watching your business grow from nothing, all while wishing it would blow up overnight.

Selling your business is a great last resort if the work becomes just too much for you or if you lose your passion for DJing. That's all right, too—you're always going to be evolving as a human being, so if DJing no longer makes you happy, it might be time to get rid of your successful business.

So, let's say you've decided to sell your DJ business to someone else. Here are a few rules to keep in mind:

- *Always have a sales agreement.* You never want to sell a business without an agreement stating how much you're selling the business for, all of the assets that you're including in the sale (which includes proprietary information such as client information and song lists), how the transition between you and the new owner would go, and a list of every single fee and cost that the buyer will have to bear. Having everything written on paper up front will avoid a lengthy legal battle later if you and the new buyer have a disagreement over the terms of the sale.
- *Price out everything, even your business's name.* One mistake that a lot of small business owners make when they sell their business is failing to charge what their name and reputation are worth. If your business has been successful enough, your business's name could be worth quite a bit aside from the cost of your equipment and your client list.
- *Transfer any equipment warranties or service contracts.* When the new owner of your DJ business takes over, she'll have to take your word that the equipment she's buying is in good enough shape to hit the ground running. If you have any service contracts or extended warranties on your DJ gear, you'll want to make sure those are included as part of the agreement so the new owners gets no surprises if something fails. Remember that lost downtime sucks, especially if you just bought the business!

Buying (and Upgrading) Gear

Buying and selling equipment are two of the best parts of being a DJ, and as we talked about in chapter 8, building the perfect DJ rig is important. Every working DJ I know loves going to equipment swap meets and conventions to find the best, newest gear on the market. As a professional DJ, you'll certainly want to upgrade your equipment as time goes on, and as you start having a higher budget for equipment by way of reinvesting in your business with your profits, you will want to get rid of the equipment that you're not using anymore. Likewise, you might want to approach other DJ professionals who are selling their gear and score good deals on equipment to help bridge the gap between where you were and where you want to be.

Every audio engineer and DJ I've ever met has been hosed on equipment by eBayers and craigslist scammers. It happens all the time, and it's not just about losing your money completely. There are reproductions of just about every piece of electronics on the market, and scammers will frequently try to sell these knock-offs as the real thing. Being aware of what to look for is important when buying and maintaining equipment.

- *Always insist on paperwork.* Ask for original receipts and any servicing paperwork. You want to make sure that any factory servicing that needs to be done can take place with minimal hassle. If you don't have the proper paperwork, getting your equipment fixed can be impossible. You'll also want to know when the equipment was purchased and get a record of any servicing it's had.
- *Make sure it works!* I know this sounds basic, but if you can, test every function. If you're buying from an online seller, make sure that the sellers backs up the claims in online advertisements.
- *Make sure the descriptions are correct.* Sometimes sellers don't realize what they have (which, when it works in your favor, is great); sometimes they overestimate their gear and list something that's actually a watered-down piece of the expensive gear you're actually looking for. Check photos carefully against descriptions and, if possible, ask for clear pictures that show model number and serial number.
- *Watch out for stolen gear.* Often shady craigslist sellers look to make a quick buck with stolen gear. As a small business owner, you don't want to be caught with stolen gear—make sure that you can verify the source of any equipment you're buying.
- *Never send a money order, and always use a traceable, refundable payment.* If you're buying online, never send a monetary instrument that you can't electronically trace and cancel. Paying by credit card via PayPal is the safest and most common method because both PayPal and your credit card company will actively pursue any fraudulent sellers who sell you gear that either doesn't function properly or doesn't arrive at your doorstep at all.
- *Last but not least, make sure the deal isn't too good to be true.* This is self-explanatory; if you're picking up a whole Rane Serato rig off eBay's via "Buy It Now" from a seller for $100, you're probably getting ripped off.

Liquidating Your Gear

We covered a lot of information regarding buying new gear; now let's talk about the flipside: liquidating your gear. Selling your equipment is hard to do. You might think your old equipment is worth a lot of money. It's hard to be objective about your equipment after you've been using it for several years and you have come to rely on it, but the truth is that your equipment probably isn't worth much within a few years and that if you try to ask nearly full retail price, you're going to be disappointed at how little interest you get.

If you're selling your gear, you need to remember a few suggestions:

■ *Always price your gear realistically.* Check eBay and find out what people are paying for same-condition DJ gear. That should be your base price, and always open yourself up to negotiations. You'll be surprised at how easy you'll sell your gear if it's represented fairly and you're friendly when negotiating with the buyer.

■ *Represent your gear truthfully.* Don't tell the buyer anything other than the absolute truth. Your gear will probably be well-used, and even if it looks new, make sure the buyer knows how long you've been using it and under what conditions. Those factors change the value quite a bit, even if your opinion might be different than fact.

■ *Be patient with your buyer's questions.* Make sure you take the time to answer every question you can as best you can. Buyers like patient sellers who can make them at ease with their purchase.

When to Quit

The last scenario you want to think about as a small business owner is quitting. I know that the very possibility probably drives you insane. However, I've watched family and friends hang on to business ventures that were bleeding them dry of both their money and their zest for life. Being a small business owner, as we talked about on the first pages of this book, is an exhilarating and liberating experience. You're a one-person show, and you're the one in charge for once. Finally! I know that it feels great to finally make it to the boss's chair, but life doesn't always go the way you want.

Businesses aren't in great shape these days. Just look at all the businesses in your neighborhood that haven't made it through this economy. We all assume that your

DJ business will be a success, but you might one day wake up and realize that you're just not interested in working as hard as you have been. Whether it's to heed health concerns or to spend more time with your family (remember that behind-the-scenes work takes just as much time, if not more, than your gigs), if you feel it's time to quit, you need to listen to your gut.

Having an internal conflict about your business? The answers to three big questions may tell you if it's time to shut down and move on to your next venture—whether it's returning to the 9-to-5 world or starting a new small business.

- *Can you financially afford to run your business any longer?* Your business might not be turning a profit; in fact, your business might be costing you out-of-pocket money that you would otherwise have in savings. If your business is generating zero useful income, you've probably got a good reason to let go. Don't let your business become a burden.
- *Is your happiness at risk?* If you're depressed because you have to go to work at your business—and it's affecting your emcee ability and your relations with your clientele—you should get out before you allow your business to collapse with a bad reputation.
- *How's your health treating you?* Is running this DJ business affecting your health? Are the constant stage shows and activity that come with being a part of a school dance or a wedding exhausting or exhilarating?

Failure Is, in Fact, an Option

Now that you've reached the end of the book, I hope your business is off to a big success. I hope that you're booked every weekend and have a constant stream of word-of-mouth customers. I hope you're on a regular diet of wedding cake and buffet line food, courtesy of your clients. But if things don't work out, and the business-building steps we talked about end up becoming too challenging for you, it's all right to give yourself permission to quit.

Don't ever feel bad about quitting when it's the best move for you or your family. Sometimes the collateral stress of living your dream can cripple your enthusiasm and cause problems in your life that make the benefits of self-employment unenjoyable.

Ultimately, it's all right to decide that this isn't for you.

Failure isn't a badge of dishonor when it comes to running your own small business as long as the end comes after your business was run in a safe, ethical manner. You can't control your market; you can't control your clients. As long as you gave 100 percent every time, there's nothing to be sorry for. If you can proudly walk away from your business and say that you gave it your best shot, you're in a fantastic position worth being proud of.

A business is a huge part of its owner's identity. Being "Jim the DJ" is part of who you are and who you've evolved into during the time when you were running your business. Losing a label that was part of your identity can be alarming and can generally make you feel remarkably uncomfortable. Remember that your friends and family will always love you for who you are, not what you are. If someone in your life focuses primarily on your work in the DJ business, that person is probably missing the true spectrum of who you are.

All this being said, I hope you find success. If you don't, maybe you can take the lessons and the skills you learned here to start a new business or go to work at another business and become a valued member of that team. If things don't work out, just know that you did your best. That's all you ever wanted to do in the first place, right?

Good luck with your new DJ business!

Appendix A: How to DJ Your Own Wedding with an iPod

All right, my new DJ business owners, now it's time to cover your ears and hide your eyes. This appendix is for people who want to do things a little differently—and these people will, indeed, be costing you money. Still, self-DJing your wedding is becoming a popular choice for many couples on a budget. Although it's a good way to achieve good results without much expenditure, in many ways DJing your own wedding could completely backfire without the help of a professional.

Self-DJing their wedding is something that many hopeful couples try to do. Unfortunately, sometimes hiring a professional is the better option—regardless of a couple's best intentions. Not understanding how a sound system works is the number one reason why self-DJed events turn out very badly—and erratic song selection is usually the number two reason.

If you're confident about taking on the challenge of DJing your own wedding, you should know a few things to make sure you're on the right track. Embarrassing yourself at your own event should be saved for after an excess of champagne, not before the evening really gets going—and an uncoordinated self-DJing effort is an easy way to embarrass yourself.

Self-DJing usually is based on an iPod—the miracle of modern technology that makes it possible to recall any song or album that's in your head and play it instantly. I love my iPod, and it travels everywhere with me, and many other people feel the same way. Bringing an iPod to an event to self-DJ is a popular choice, but there are a few general rules to remember.

- **Have your playlists in order.** Be sure that your playlists are ready to go and that the songs flow together well. Make sure your songs are genre-appropriate and sound good (meaning they all have the highest-quality encoding possible), and make sure your songs are of equal volume. Turning off features such as iTunes volume limiting and "enhancement" will go a long way toward consistent playback. Despite their innocent-sounding names, these features can hinder the sound of your playback in a large system.

■ **Be prepared with cabling.** The most common cable you will need is a $\frac{1}{8}$-inch miniconnector (headphone connector) to RCA plugs. You may also need $\frac{1}{8}$-inch mini-to-dual $\frac{1}{4}$-inch phono jacks; it depends on the mixer and sound system you're using. You'll plug this cable into the "stereo return" or "line in" section of your sound system's mixer. You may also need a "DI," or "direct injection" box if your sound system's mixer isn't equipped with line-level inputs. This box—either in one stereo or a dual mono configuration—will allow you to plug your iPod's high-output line level connection into the lower-level, commonly used microphone-level inputs on most mixers.

■ **Watch your volume.** You should rely on your mixer, not your iPod's relatively weak and noisy headphone amplifier, to push the largest amount of volume. Because the iPod doesn't have a built-in low-level output (unless you count going from your dock connector, which requires a special adapter), you need to do a careful balancing act between what output you're feeding the gear and what it's calibrated to handle. Too loud on your iPod output, and you'll distort the signal going into the mixer. Too little, and your mixer will introduce lots of noise to your signal. Products such as the FiiO L3 ($10) allow you to connect the dock connector of your iPod to the mixer at line level—and is the easiest and cheapest way to make sure you're not over-driving your signal.

■ **Always rely on a direct connection from your iPod to your mixer.** Don't fall into the common trap of using a microphone to mic a speaker on a desktop playback system—that doesn't work and makes you look like a fool to anyone who knows audio. Always rely on direct, solid connections.

■ **Watch your power!** You should never trust your iPod's battery life on a signal charge for an important event; always use a stable power supply and plug in your iPod to prevent losing power in the middle of an important song.

■ **Lastly, never be afraid to hire a professional.** Pro DJs know how sound reinforcement works, and they can also give you an expert-level emcee experience, something you may not have time to do when you're in charge of your own event.

Appendix B: Sound Reinforcement Reference Manual

Mixing live sound is one of the most frustrating processes for new audio engineers to learn. The principles are similar to studio work, yet some of the rules are completely different. You might need a lot of knowledge while in the field with your new DJ rig—and this appendix can help you.

Here are some common problems you might run into when you're setting up your DJ rig. This reference will help you find a good solution—and remember that practice makes perfect.

How to EQ a Room

Start with your rack or system processing EQ flat across the spectrum. You may use an RTA—real-time analyzer—for this process, but it's not mandatory. You should always equalize your room with material that you're used to hearing and that you know well; that way you can judge when your system sounds correct.

How's the lower mid-range in the vocals and instruments? Starting with your lower-mid-range frequencies, back off the areas surrounding 350Hz to 500Hz. These are the trouble areas that are mostly responsible for nasal, mid-range-heavy sounds within your mix. Your speaker system may be responding properly, but the room is creating issues. This frequency range will help tailor the speaker system to deliver clearer vocals and instrument passages. This clears the way for a deep, solid low end with a sparkly, clear-but-not-obnoxious high range.

Speaking of your high frequencies, how's the sibilance in your mix? Generally, vocal sibilance—from either recorded material or your vocal microphones—is centered around 1.5kHz to 3kHz. You'll need to gradually back off in these frequency ranges if you notice that crispy, harsh vowel sound in your speakers.

EQing a room for low end is a different animal completely. If your speakers are crossed over correctly, you might not have to do much EQ work at all; if they're not, or if you're not using separate subwoofers, you might have to increase some gain around 60Hz to add some "thump" to your mix.

When using EQ in a room, remember a few basic tips:

- Subtract EQ frequencies slowly and cautiously; it's really easy to kill the tone and timbre of your mix when you use subtractive EQ too liberally. When adding EQ, be even more careful: Adding frequencies too haphazardly can cause feedback and blown speakers if you push it too hard, and that's relatively easy to do on some systems. You might find, if you scoop out too much, say, 250Hz, that saxophones and male vocals seem not to sit right in the room. That's problematic—make sure you don't make too much corrective EQ without paying attention to how it harms the overall picture.

Room EQ Reference

Problem Adjustment	Typical Frequency
Nasal, narrow mid-range	Reduce 250Hz to 500Hz; add 10K
Harsh highs	Reduce 1.25kHz, 3–3.5kHz, 6.3kHz
Lack of bass impact, fluid bass	Add 60Hz to 80Hz gradually, subtract 250
Too much low-end distortion	Reduce 100Hz and below, check crossover
Vocal sibilance	Focus reduction at 3kHz
Vocals buried in mix	Add gently 1kHz to 3kHz; reduce loudest ranges

- Don't use cheap EQ. Cheap EQ units tend not to be as accurate as their slightly more expensive counterparts; in fact, cheap EQs are prone to a phenomenon known as "pot stretch." As the unit heats up and expands electronically, the circuits lose their accuracy. This can result in a muddy, undefined sound.
- EQ isn't always the answer. Before resorting to room-tuning EQ, try repositioning your speakers or making sure that your cables are in good order. Sometimes faulty cables can cause a drop in quality frequency response.

Feedback Removal

Symptom	Fix
High-pitched feedback	Reduce selectively: 1kHz to 6.3kHz
Very high-pitched feedback	Reduce selectively: 12kHz and up
Low-end feedback	Reduce 100Hz and below in a downward slope; verify proper hand positioning (not over the ball)

Fighting Microphone Feedback

One of the most frustrating problems for new sound engineers is vocal feedback, and it's a problem you'll have as a DJ when you bring your microphone out for announcements. Making sure that your microphone doesn't feed back during announcements—or, worse, important toasts or speeches—is a huge priority in your live sound rig.

Here's a quick guide to removing vocal feedback. You should always try some small adjustments on your vocal channel first; then, if you're still having the problem, try adjusting with your house EQ.

Troubleshooting a System

As we talked about earlier, in basic signal flow, there's always a procedure to follow when you need to troubleshoot something. See the worksheet on the next page for troubleshooting common sound system problems.

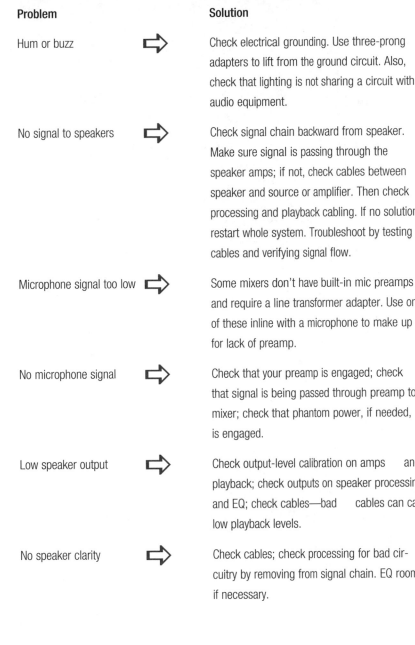

Problem		Solution
Hum or buzz	⇨	Check electrical grounding. Use three-prong adapters to lift from the ground circuit. Also, check that lighting is not sharing a circuit with audio equipment.
No signal to speakers	⇨	Check signal chain backward from speaker. Make sure signal is passing through the speaker amps; if not, check cables between speaker and source or amplifier. Then check processing and playback cabling. If no solution, restart whole system. Troubleshoot by testing cables and verifying signal flow.
Microphone signal too low	⇨	Some mixers don't have built-in mic preamps and require a line transformer adapter. Use one of these inline with a microphone to make up for lack of preamp.
No microphone signal	⇨	Check that your preamp is engaged; check that signal is being passed through preamp to mixer; check that phantom power, if needed, is engaged.
Low speaker output	⇨	Check output-level calibration on amps and playback; check outputs on speaker processing and EQ; check cables—bad cables can cause low playback levels.
No speaker clarity	⇨	Check cables; check processing for bad circuitry by removing from signal chain. EQ room if necessary.

Live Sound Survival Kit Checklist

Think you're ready for your first live gig? Here's a checklist of some must-have accessories for every live sound rig—stuff you'll use every night and some you'll be glad you have when things go terribly wrong.

❏ *Tool kit.* You never know when you'll need to make a repair in the field. Make sure you have several different-size screwdrivers, including a precision set.

❏ *Soldering iron and solder.* Learning how to solder and repair cables are two of the best cost-saving measures any DJ business can learn.

❏ *Gaffer's tape, in black and white.* Gaffer's tape is the stronger-yet-softer cousin of gray duct tape; it's useful for taping down cables and equipment because it doesn't leave behind a sticky residue when removed. Get two colors to help blend in to any decor—your clients will thank you.

❏ *A good flashlight.* Invest in a high-candlepower LED flashlight small enough to keep in your tool kit. You'll be surprised at how many venues supply poor lighting.

❏ *A multimeter/volt meter.* If you're having problems with your rig, it might be because you're plugged in to bad power. Use a multimeter to check how good and stable the power is in your venue.

❏ *A power grounding tester.* A grounding tester is a small, plug-size electrical device, available cheaply, which shows you if your electrical outlets are wired properly; this device is especially useful when diagnosing phantom noises in your system brought on by power grounding issues.

❏ *Spare cables.* This goes without saying, but never chance a gig without spare cables.

Appendix C: DJ Song List

As a brand new DJ business, you'll learn quickly that your business is very dynamic—the tastes of your clients change drastically over time in some ways, while some classics and one-hit-wonders always seem to still sneak into rotation. This sample song list is made from statistics collected from DJ Intelligence, one of the top full-service DJ support software companies, alongside data from *Mobile Beat Magazine*. At press time of this book, these were the top 200 requested songs and while this is a great starting point, always consult an up-to-date source when considering what songs to add to your general rotation. A great resource for updates is *Mobile Beat Magazine*'s website (www.mobilebeat.com), which features a full "Top Songs" list updated frequently.

Top 200 DJ Songs (Fall 2011)

1. Black Eyed Peas—I Gotta Feeling
2. Journey—Don't Stop Believin'
3. Lady Gaga featuring Colby O'Donis—Just Dance
4. AC/DC—You Shook Me All Night Long
5. Bon Jovi—Livin' On A Prayer
6. Beyoncé—Single Ladies (Put A Ring On It)
7. Cupid—Cupid Shuffle
8. Neil Diamond—Sweet Caroline (Good Times Never Seemed So Good)
9. Van Morrison—Brown Eyed Girl
10. Def Leppard—Pour Some Sugar On Me

11. B-52's—Love Shack
12. Usher featuring Will.I.Am—OMG
13. Michael Jackson—Billie Jean
14. DJ Casper—Cha Cha Slide
15. Lynyrd Skynyrd—Sweet Home Alabama
16. Lady Gaga—Poker Face
17. Outkast—Hey Ya!
18. ABBA—Dancing Queen
19. Usher featuring Ludacris & Lil' Jon—Yeah
20. Black Eyed Peas—Boom Boom Pow
21. Eric Clapton—Wonderful Tonight
22. The Beatles—Twist And Shout
23. Sister Sledge—We Are Family
24. Sir Mix-A-Lot—Baby Got Back
25. Kool & The Gang—Celebration
26. Justin Timberlake—Sexyback
27. Rihanna—Don't Stop The Music
28. Chris Brown—Forever
29. Bruno Mars—Just The Way You Are
30. Isley Brothers—Shout
31. Michael Jackson—Thriller
32. Pink—Raise Your Glass
33. Garth Brooks—Friends In Low Places
34. Frank Sinatra—The Way You Look Tonight
35. Jason Mraz—I'm Yours
36. The Temptations—My Girl
37. Black Eyed Peas—Let's Get It Started
38. Taio Cruz—Dynamite
39. Etta James—At Last
40. Vanilla Ice—Ice Ice Baby
41. Katy Perry—Firework
42. Foundations—Build Me Up Buttercup
43. Bob Seger & The Silver Bullet Band—Old Time Rock & Roll
44. Lady Gaga—Bad Romance
45. Michael Jackson—Don't Stop 'Til You Get Enough

46. Ke$Ha—Tik Tok

47. Kenny Loggins—Footloose

48. Flo Rida featuring T-Pain—Low

49. Commodores—Brick House

50. Flo Rida featuring David Guetta—Club Can't Handle Me

51. Elvis Presley—Can't Help Falling In Love

52. Louis Armstrong—What A Wonderful World

53. Village People—Y.M.C.A.

54. Rihanna—Only Girl (In The World)

55. Bee Gees—Stayin' Alive

56. Big & Rich—Save A Horse (Ride A Cowboy)

57. Usher—DJ Got Us Fallin' In Love

58. Righteous Brothers—Unchained Melody

59. Bryan Adams—Summer Of '69

60. Cyndi Lauper—Girls Just Want To Have Fun

61. Wild Cherry—Play That Funky Music

62. Beyoncé featuring Jay-Z—Crazy In Love

63. Jennifer Lopez featuring Pitbull—On The Floor

64. Miley Cyrus—Party In The U.S.A.

65. Train—Marry Me

66. Dexy's Midnight Runners—Come On Eileen

67. Aerosmith—I Don't Want To Miss A Thing

68. Black Eyed Peas—The Time (Dirty Bit)

69. Michael Jackson—P.Y.T. (Pretty Young Thing)

70. Michael Jackson—The Way You Make Me Feel

71. Rascal Flatts—Bless The Broken Road

72. Lonestar—Amazed

73. Jason Mraz & Colbie Caillat—Lucky

74. LMFAO featuring Lauren Bennett And GoonRock—Party Rock Anthem

75. Rednex—Cotton Eye Joe

76. Kid Rock—All Summer Long

77. House Of Pain—Jump Around

78. Michael Bublé—Everything

79. Jay-Z featuring Alicia Keys—Empire State Of Mind

80. Zac Brown Band—Chicken Fried

81. Earth, Wind & Fire—September
82. Train—Hey Soul Sister
83. Rick Springfield—Jessie's Girl
84. Enrique Iglesias featuring Pitbull—I Like It
85. Flo Rida featuring Keisha—Right Round
86. Pitbull featuring Ne-Yo, Afrojack & Nayer—Give Me Everything
87. Queen—Crazy Little Thing Called Love
88. Jack Johnson—Better Together
89. Michael Jackson—Beat It
90. Cascada—Evacuate The Dancefloor
91. Young M.C. —Bust A Move
92. Cee Lo Green—Forget You
93. Journey—Faithfully
94. Black Eyed Peas—Imma Be
95. Guns N' Roses—Sweet Child O' Mine
96. Marcia Griffiths—Electric Boogie
97. Katy Perry—Teenage Dream
98. Michael Franti & Spearhead—Say Hey (I Love You)
99. Far East Movement featuring The Cataracs & Dev—Like A G6
100. LMFAO featuring Lil Jon—Shots
101. Trey Songz featuring Nicki Minaj—Bottoms Up
102. Bill Medley & Jennifer Warnes—(I've Had) The Time Of My Life
103. Pink—Get The Party Started
104. 50 Cent—In Da Club
105. Ke$Ha—Your Love Is My Drug
106. Four Tops—I Can't Help Myself (Sugar Pie, Honey Bunch)
107. Nelly—Hot In Herre
108. Whitney Houston—I Wanna Dance With Somebody (Who Loves Me)
109. Romantics—What I Like About You
110. Chubby Checker—The Twist
111. Kings Of Leon—Sex On Fire
112. David Guetta featuring Akon—Sexy Chick
113. Norah Jones—Come Away With Me
114. Michael Bublé— Save The Last Dance For Me
115. Salt-N-Pepa—Push It

116. The Beatles—All You Need Is Love

117. KC & The Sunshine Band—Get Down Tonight

118. Al Green—Let's Stay Together

119. Cheap Trick—I Want You To Want Me

120. James Taylor—How Sweet It Is (To Be Loved By You)

121. Frank Sinatra—Fly Me To The Moon

122. Katy Perry—California Gurls

123. Prince—Kiss

124. Tim McGraw with Faith Hill—It's Your Love

125. Brooks & Dunn—Boot Scootin' Boogie

126. Taylor Swift—Love Story

127. Brad Paisley—She's Everything

128. Sugarland—Stuck Like Glue

129. U2—Beautiful Day

130. Ke$Ha—Blow

131. Madonna—Like A Prayer

132. Chris Brown—Yeah 3x

133. Lady Gaga—Born This Way

134. Lady Gaga featuring Beyoncé—Telephone

135. Brad Paisley—Then

136. California Swag District—Teach Me How To Dougie

137. Jimmy Buffett—Margaritaville

138. Los Del Rio—Macarena

139. Jackson 5—ABC

140. Rascal Flatts—My Wish

141. M.C. Hammer—U Can't Touch This

142. Kanye West featuring Jamie Foxx—Gold Digger

143. Marvin Gaye—Let's Get It On

144. John Travolta & Olivia Newton-John—Grease Megamix

145. Bryan Adams—(Everything I Do) I Do It For You

146. Aretha Franklin—Respect

147. Pitbull featuring T-Pain—Hey Baby (Drop It To The Floor)

148. Ke$Ha—We R Who We R

149. Black Eyed Peas—Rock That Body

150. Adele—Rolling In The Deep

151. Aerosmith—Walk This Way
152. Black Eyed Peas—My Humps
153. Johnny Cash—Ring Of Fire
154. K-Ci & Jojo—All My Life
155. Billy Idol—White Wedding
156. Daft Punk—One More Time
157. UB40—Red Red Wine
158. Tim McGraw—My Best Friend
159. Rihanna—Disturbia
160. Rascal Flatts—Life Is A Highway
161. Enrique Iglesias featuring Ludacris—Tonight (I'm Lovin' You)
162. Gloria Gaynor—I Will Survive
163. a-ha—Take On Me
164. Big & Rich—Lost In This Moment
165. Coldplay—Viva La Vida
166. Katy Perry—Hot N Cold
167. Dion—Runaround Sue
168. Rihanna—Rude Boy
169. Lifehouse—You And Me
170. Rihanna featuring Jay-Z—Umbrella
171. Will Smith—Gettin' Jiggy Wit It
172. Violent Femmes—Blister In The Sun
173. Justin Timberlake—Rock Your Body
174. Sorta Crackers Band—Chicken Dance
175. Dean Martin—That's Amore
176. Eagles—Hotel California
177. Queen—Another One Bites The Dust
178. Prince—1999
179. Billy Idol—Mony Mony
180. Rihanna—S&M
181. B.O.B. featuring Bruno Mars—Nothin' On You
182. Kings Of Leon—Use Somebody
183. Black Eyed Peas—Just Can't Get Enough
184. Jay Sean featuring Lil Wayne—Down
185. Frank Sinatra—Come Fly With Me

186. Grandmaster Slice—Electric Slide
187. Chubby Checker—Let's Twist Again
188. Lady Gaga—Alejandro
189. The Beatles—I Saw Her Standing There
190. Barry White—Can't Get Enough Of Your Love, Babe
191. Percy Sledge—When A Man Loves A Woman
192. T.I. —Whatever You Like
193. Temptations—Ain't Too Proud To Beg
194. Weather Girls—It's Raining Men
195. George Strait—I Cross My Heart
196. Sean Kingston—Fire Burning
197. Edward Maya featuring Vika Jigulina—Stereo Love
198. Digital Underground—The Humpty Dance
199. Gnarls Barkley—Crazy
200. Tone Lōc—Wild Thing

Index

product standards and, 136–37
   rates and, 63
   for wedding entertainment, 13
complaints, 49–51
conflict management, 122–23
connectors, 95
contracts, 59–61, 70
control boards, lighting, 103
controllers, light, 103
corporations, 21, 31, 57–58
cosigners, 54
country music, 44
coupons, 48–49
craigslist, 48, 85, 140
credit, 32, 33, 53–54, 68
credit cards, 34, 54
crossfaders, 80
crossovers, 91
crowd control, 122–23

D

dba (doing business as), 31, 57
demographics, 111–13, 122
demos, 41–44
deposits, 34, 64, 66
digital equalizers, 97
Digital Multiplex (DMX) control, 103, 104
digital signal processors (DSPs), 88, 90
digital song storage, 82–83, 105
digital systems, 78, 79
dinner music, 43
directory listings, 32
discipline, 2, 5
discounts and promotions, 46, 48–49
diversity of music, 33, 40, 41, 43–44, 78
DJ businesses, overview
   benefits, 3, 6, 9
   expansion of, 138
   job description, 1, 3–4, 9
   quitting, 8, 141–43
   and reputation, 135–36
   sales of, 138–39
   timeline and plan, 10

DJ Forums, 47
"DJ in a box" systems, 77
DJ Jukebox (software), 82
DMX (Digital Multiplex) control, 103, 104
doing business as (dba), 31, 57
dress, 117–18
drivers, 91
drugs, 115–16, 118
DSPs (digital signal processors), 88, 90
dual-drivers, 91

E

earplugs, 94
eBay, 58–59, 84, 85, 140
EIN (employer identification number), 30, 34, 57, 74
emcee (MC) duties
   announcements, 122
   competition and quality of, 137
   crowd control, 122–23
   dress and appearance, 117–18
   etiquette guidelines, 116–17
   introductions, 117
   live band competition and, 41
   overview, 114–15
   scripts and rehearsals, 118–19, 120–21
   song requests, 119, 122
   video demos featuring, 43
employees, 74
employer identification number (EIN), 30, 34, 57, 74
endgame plans, 8, 139–43
EQ, 80, 88, 96–97
equipment. *See also* sound equipment
   air travel and, 81
   analog *versus* digital, 78–79
   backups, 83–84
   hearing safety, 94
   insurance for, 55–56
   lighting systems, 101–4
   maintenance of, 89
   mixers, 80–81
   overview, 77–78

introductions, 117
invoicing, 64–65
IRS (Internal Revenue Service), 30, 67, 68, 69, 74.
    See also taxes

K
kilohertz, 91

L
last call, 44
lawsuits, 64
LED lights, 101–2
legal issues
    attorneys, 31, 58–59
    business fees, 56—57
    business registration, 30–31
    business structure, 20, 21, 30, 31, 57–58
    contracts, 59–61, 70
    document storage, 70
    insurance, 55–56
    nonpaying clients, 59, 64
    piracy, 109, 110
    as self-employment responsibility, 6
    trademarks, 31
liabilities, 69–71
liability insurance, 55
lighting, 101–4
limited liability corporations (LLC), 21, 31, 57–58
loans, 11, 12, 18, 53–54, 68, 69
logos, 31
lossless compression, 111

M
market analysis
    analog *versus* digital systems and, 78
    business plans featuring, 22–23
    event types, 13–14
    and marketing strategies, 36–39
    song selection and, 111–13
marketing
    business name selection, 30
    competition analysis, 39–41
    market analysis and targeting, 36–39
    online advertising, 45–49
    reputation management, 49–51
    as self-employment responsibility, 6
    start-up budgets, 11, 12
master of ceremonies. *See* emcee (MC) duties
microphones, 98–99
mixers, 80–81
monitor mixes, 81
motivation, 5
MP3, 109, 110–11
Murray, Jean, 2
music
    digital song storage, 82–83, 105
    live bands, as competition, 39–41
    records, vinyl, 78, 79, 80
    song lists, 41, 105–13, 137
    sourcing *versus* piracy, 109–10
    variety of, 33, 40, 41, 43–44, 78
music charts, 107–8
My DJ Space (forum), 47
Myspace, 46, 49

N
names, business, 29–30, 31–32, 34
networking, 56
nonmusical entertainment, as competition, 13

O
omnidirectional microphones, 98–99
Our DJ Talk (forum), 47
outros, 44

P
parabolic stage lights (par cans), 101–2
parent dances, 44
partnerships, 21, 31
passive speakers, 92
payments, 34–35, 69
PayPal, 34, 84, 140
phone numbers, 32
phones, 72

piracy, 109, 110
pitch control, 79
pop music, 43
prefader sends, 81
pricing, 62–64, 100, 133
Prodigy, 47
Pro DJ Forums, 47
professionalism
   business name selection and, 30
   dress and appearance, 117–18
   in online advertising, 47
   reputation management and, 49–51, 135–36
   substance abuse and, 115–16, 118
   video demos and, 41, 42, 44
Promo Only, 110

Q
quality of service, 37, 136–37

R
radio frequency interference, 99–100
rates, 62–64
R&B music, 44
real-time analyzer (RTA), 96, 97
record keeping, 68–71
records, vinyl, 78, 79, 80
refractor lights, 102–3
registration, business, 30–31
rehearsals, 64, 118–19
rental equipment, 56, 64, 100
reputation management, 49–51, 135–36
reviews, negative, 49–51, 135–36
RIAA EQ, 80
road cases, 81–82
rock and roll music, 44
room acoustics, 96–97
royal weddings, 127
RPM drives, 83

S
safety, 94, 104
SBA (Small Business Administration), 57, 135
schedules, 5
scripts, 118–19
self-employment and small businesses, overview
   benefits of, 1
   challenges, 2–3, 4
   description, 4, 6
   failure rate statistics, 135
   field experience statistics, 3
   financial assessment worksheets, 7
   operations timeline, 12
   personal priorities assessments, 3–4
   profitability and average income statistics, 2
   start-up timeline, 2
   time management tips, 5
selling
   business, 138–39
   equipment, 85
service fees, 34
SHN files, 111
signal flow, 87–90
Small Business Administration (SBA), 57, 135
small businesses. *See* self-employment and small
    businesses, overview
smoking, 118
social networking, 45–47, 49
SoftJock's Remote Request (software), 122
software
   digital storage, 82–83
   music requests organization, 122
sole proprietorship, 21, 31, 57
song lists, 41, 105–13, 137
sound
   factors affecting, 97
   live, 86–87
   updating, 137
soundboard recordings, 42
sound equipment
   cables, 93, 94–95
   EQ and acoustics, 96–97

About the Author

Joe Shambro is an audio engineer, production consultant, and technology writer from St. Louis, Missouri. His live sound and studio engineering clientele includes several Grammy-winning artists alongside many top-level independent musicians. He also works closely with corporate clients and government organizations, including such entities as the United States Air Force and NASA. He has recorded and mixed a wide variety of projects, traveling worldwide as a live sound engineer; his recording and mixing work has been featured on outlets such as NPR, The Armed Forces Network, Clear Channel Radio, NBC, and CNN.

Joe is also the Home Recording Guide for The New York Times Company's About.com website and a contributing writer for *EQ Magazine*. His first book, *How to Start a Home-based Recording Studio Business*, was released by Globe Pequot Press in 2010.